THE LAZY GARDENER

Dedication

As with everything I do, this book was a co-production with my wife Marea, whose acid wit, cutting tongue and relentless support saw the job through.

THE LAZY GARDENER

DON BURKE

NEW HOLLAND

Contents

Introduction

The Good Oil

Well troops, it's a quarter of a bloody century since the original *Lazy Gardener* book was inflicted on a largely unsuspecting mob of backyard bludgers: you lot (or maybe your parents).

So maybe it's time to re-think gardening. According to the Oxford English Dictionary, gardening is: 'A boring, pedantic discipline whereby lonely people grow plants to fill the vast void in their social lives'. To me, it's comfy chairs around a huge table, some friends, good food and wine outdoors in the sun. It's the joy of casually plucking some variegated applemint or coriander leaves from the pot nearby to garnish your goulash. It's also the joy of watching the kids making mud pies and having adventures in their own enchanted forest.

But above and beyond all else, it is cheating. All good gardeners are cheats and liars. They make a boring flat backyard look like a Balinese tropical jungle or a French provincial farm. It's not magic, it's cheating and trickery. Then they lie about how hard it was to create. It's dead easy and, even though I will get expelled from the Royal Horticultural Society for telling you our secret and mysterious ways, I will herein reveal all the secrets we use to impress everyone.

While on the subject of cheating and lying, we will also look at the environment and r'cycling (non-trendies please replace the apostrophe with an e). With the deepest of respect for those dedicated to this noble cause, we will do two sections: the current environmental practices (r'cycling, water tanks, etc.) and the second bit where we tell the truth. I strongly advise trendies to ignore the second section as it may offend.

CHAPTER 1
The Castle

*T*he sweetest moments in life are often so simple. A hug from your two-year-old son or daughter. A caring touch on the shoulder from your partner. The dog putting his head on your lap. Or watching the spring leaves unfold on a Japanese maple.

These simple things seem to make everything worthwhile. But then you hop in the car and someone gives you the finger. Road rage and hatred for each other is out there on the highways. Like rottweilers in cages, car drivers are angry and potentially dangerous.

Everyone works long hours. Working mums slave away to pay for the child-minding fees so they have time to work so they can pay for the child minding fees. Huge mortgages hang over our heads and there is so much to do. Even holidays are stressful times. Jetting away to Thailand, endless holiday planning and queuing at airports. Race here, race there, race back. How was your holiday? A bloody blur to me, mate.

So you turn to your own place. The Castle. This is the last bastion of sanity. The fortification of friendliness. The rampart of relaxation. Your own Xanadu. If Kubla Khan can decree 'A stately pleasure dome', why not you?

Where Alph, the sacred river, ran
Through caverns measureless to man
Down to a sunless sea.
So twice five miles of fertile ground
With walls and towers were girdled round:
And there were gardens bright with sinuous rills,
Where blossomed many an incense-bearing tree;
And here were forests ancient as the hills,
Enfolding sunny spots of greenery.

This book is written for you. This is your guide to constructing your dome of pleasure. And the purest of all pleasures is indolence. A woozy afternoon lazing around a table in the backyard with your best friends: Hahn Light, Jacob's Creek and Adrienne and Paddo. Exquisite moments as Madison and Morgan fill a plastic wheelbarrow with magic flowers while Tyler and Connor are excavating their secret bunker under the weeping mulberry. These friendships will last a lifetime and the memories even longer.

This is what gardening is all about. It is not about fiendishly hard work, nor is it about being a slave to your garden. It is about designing a fantasy area that really provides a home and hearth for the family. A magic area where you feel safe and happy. Where maybe you grow organic vegies, maybe even have some chooks. It almost certainly involves a transitional zone at the back of the house that is both indoors and outdoors: an entertaining area, a wet-day play area for the kids or just a kickback area for Mum and Dad.

In the chapter on Fantasies, you hopefully will find the inspiration for your dream. And the words 'your dream' are everything. Nothing is as exhilarating or as quietly triumphant as seeing your own design come to fruition. In that regard, I hope you will understand my self-indulgence in including my own designs and ideas in this book. Like everyone, I love my own designs best. I hope my enthusiasm for these designs will encourage you to try out your own hand.

If, like me, most of your life's artistic endeavours were confined to kindy when you did superb finger-paintings—perhaps it's time to create anew. I was the Vincent van Gogh of this fine art form, finger-painting. Like him, I was never appreciated at the time. Like all of us, most of my life has seen the frustrated artiste stifled by the daily grind.

So, it will emerge in this book that gardens are neither about grandiose designs, nor about flowers, paving or pots. Great gardens are about people. Be wary of the garden designer who works to create garden designs for his or her portfolio. Often ultra-modern gardens look great in a photo, but are miserable places to live in. Stick to your own dreams.

Through this paltry little book, we'll look at how to fulfil your dreams easily. Simple ways to cheat. Simple ways to create wonderful effects that look like a tropical rainforest in suburbia or a kid's fairy garden in the inner city.

We will debunk the Old Husbands' Tales and look at low-maintenance, environmentally friendly gardening. Along the way,

I hope you'll get a giggle as we look at how silly we all can be. I hope you'll forgive me for getting on my horse, grabbing my lance and charging at a few windmills. This book, as its predecessor published in 1983 did, will rattle your cage a bit.

This is no re-write of the original 1983 book of *The Lazy Gardener* though. It's a totally new look at gardens and gardening today. Much has changed since 1983. So there are new jokes, new poems, new chapters, even a new dog–Clyde. Woof, on the cover of most of the editions of the first book, died in 1996 at the age of 12. We still miss him and his impeccable manners–he was like Alfred, the patient butler from *Batman*.

Clyde is an unregistered Tenterfield Terrier (aka mini foxie). He came from stray parents that colonised a farm in Jamberoo, New South Wales. Clyde is an opportunist and a scrounger, but seriously smart. Pets, including dogs, are an essential part of a great garden, so they too appear in this book.

I hope this book gives you some useful ideas for your garden. I hope it helps you realise that gardening is simple and fun: that all of the complex stuff you read is nonsense. That garden design is simple and that your own designs can be exquisite. But whatever, your design is the best one in the world–for you.

And to everyone, thanks a lot for the support over the past quarter of a century: they have been the best years of my life.

Left: The original Lazy Gardener book published in 1983.

Clyde is an opportunist and seriously smart.

CHAPTER 2
Getting it right

Clarrie is a dedicated gardener and handyman. He retired last year from his job as sandwich-hand at the canteen at OCD Enterprises. He has the perfect garage: his EH Holden, Pearl's Austin A40 (which has still only done 143 miles) and his workshop. Clarrie has the world's largest collection of Moccona coffee bottles, some 3700 bottles in all, each filled with nails or screws or hinges or irrigation fittings or electrical bits and pieces or bolts or spares for his tools.

There might be 3700 jars, but Clarrie knows exactly where each and every screw, hinge or fitting is located. Inside his head is the complete layout of his entire workshop. On his pegboard are the ghostly outlines of pliers, hammers, screwdrivers, bolt cutters, secateurs and dozens of other tools. Inside each outline is the precise tool that the outline was drawn around. Every spade, fork, rake, shovel, broom, axe, mattock and crowbar has its exact location too.

Clarrie spends countless hours sharpening and oiling his tools. His bench is kept as clean as a hospital's operating theatre. The wooden handles of his garden tools are as well oiled and intact as they were when his great-grandfather passed them on to his grandfather.

Each year he accidentally lets slip the name of the new piece of electrical equipment he needs to complete his workshop. In the last 10 years, Pearl or the kids have given him a router, a bench-grinder, a power saw, a cordless drill, a kanga hammer and a power nail gun. His spare batteries sit in exquisitely lined-up battery chargers. This year he needs a new blower.

Clarrie is a very happy man and Pearl is just as happy. She has her frog collection (5783 of them—all green) her teaspoon collection, which supports her world map with each of her *Women's Weekly* World Discovery Tour routes marked on it. Pearl is deeply involved in her patchwork quilts. She is modestly regarded as the Leonardo da Vinci of quilt making, although she would never admit to this title. They have separate bedrooms now so that Pearl's incessant tapping of her thimbled finger on the needles doesn't wake Clarrie. He goes to bed by 6.30pm each night so that he can rise by 5am to start in his workshop. Pearl and her Father O'Leary's Cappuccino liqueur often stay up til 1 or 2am after which she does Sudoku until dawn.

Their lives are complete: utterly, deliriously happy. Theirs is the ultimate relationship–a marriage by avoidance. They can go months without even seeing each other. But they are both very busy and love gardening. She has her African violet collection all with wick pots. He has his vegie garden which fills the entire backyard: gridded, fertilised and staked very, very precisely. Each stake sporting the Yates seed packet at the top.

Gardening is all about good habits. I am sure that you, dear reader, venture out into the streets each autumn with your wheelbarrow, shovel and broom. Soon to return with your expedition's treasure: thousands of leaves for the compost bin. Perhaps you return more than a little troubled that your neighbours chuck these gems away.

Composting is its own reward. A biological layer-cake of putrefaction. Each composter has his or her own jealously guarded recipe. I usually do a series of 100mm layers:

1. Dead leaves
2. Kitchen scraps (avoid rat-attractors like corn)
3. Weeds (not bulbous weeds like onion weed or oxalis)
4. Prunings
5. Lawn clippings

It's a good idea to add some compost activator every layer or two: it's called garden soil.

The big mistake most people make is that they don't turn their heap. Turning to produce aeration is very important. So, get two large plastic bins with the open bottom – and sit them on the ground. Every few weeks (or more often) pull the bin off the contents (they lift off like a sand castle bucket). Now shovel it all back in. This aerates the mix and gives you a six-pack.

Turning the compost heap.

This will break down in two or three months in summer or four or five months in winter. I can't get near my bin at the moment though. It's winter and the blue wrens (Superb Fairy-wrens for the pedants) are queued-up six deep, eating the flying insects that are breeding in their thousands in the warmth of the compost. As each flight of insects leaves through cracks between the lid and the bin, the wrens swarm all over them. So tame are these birds that they even land on my shoulders or back if I keep very still. This to me is what gardening is about. Without my compost bins, many of these wrens would have starved. As I open the lid, they dart in for dinner or land on my shoulders to grab a morsel from the air.

Weeks later, this compost is used as a soil conditioner, as a surface mulch or as an ingredient in potting mixes. I remove some of the worms, beetle larvae and even centipedes to feed to my aviary birds and the chooks. Many of our kitchen scraps go to the chooks: lettuce, fruit, corn, rice, bread, silverbeet (anything green), mango skins, etc.

About three times a year I shovel their soil/poo mix onto the vegie garden. I couldn't tell you how many times we have reconsumed our own food or scraps. Through the chooks, through the soil, through us, through the chooks, through the soil, etc.

Tools

Tools should last forever. Mine bring back memories of my dad, his dad and his dad. My shovels and forks touch my roots at both ends.

- Never leave your tools out in the rain or leaning against the outside of the house.
- Always oil their blades (I use old motor oil or bits of leftover oil) with your oil can and an old rag. It's important to oil saw blades in particular.
- Always oil the wooden handles of your tools with 50/50 linseed oil and mineral turps. I leave it permanently mixed up in an old peanut-butter jar. Paint it on with an old brush that is no good for painting any more.

Oil your saw blades using an old rag and old motor oil or bits of leftover oil.

Just squirt on a bit of the oil and rub it in.

Oil wooden handles with a half-and-half mix of linseed oil and mineral turps.

My mix, in an old peanut butter jar, is permanently mixed up and ready to use.

A: Using a bench grinder to sharpen your spade is a perfect rainy day job.

B: A spade sharpened to perfection.

A: One of my favourite tools, a Swiss Istor sharpener.

B: Simply run the Swiss Istor along your secateur blades as if you are peeling a potato. You will be amazed how sharp your secateurs will become after just a few passes.

- Use your bench grinder to sharpen spades (yes, they are a cutting implement), hedge trimmers, bolsters, stone chisels, axes, tomahawks, mattocks, etc.
- Regularly sharpen wood chisels with a hand-operated grinding stone.
- Regularly sharpen your secateurs. I use a Swiss Istor sharpener— this is the best tool I have ever used: www.swissistorsharpener. com.au. Stand all hardened paintbrushes in paint stripper. When they soften, wash them well and put them away for re-use.

Save all of these jobs for a rainy day. It's so satisfying to get it done.

Hoses

Respect your hoses. They cost around $40 to $80 so letting them disintegrate is very costly. I suggest that expensive long-lasting, kink-free are the best value for money. Don't buy cheapies. A few tips:

- Never coil or wind up your hose. This leads to kinking when you roll it out. Lay your garden hoses along the lawn/garden edges so they are ready to use.
- Never mix your brands. Select one brand–eg. Gardena, and buy that one all the time. Why? Because they are all slightly different in diameter and tend to blow apart when you mix different brands of fittings.
- Always keep spare fittings on hand.
- Get a packet of 'O' rings to repair fittings. These are the rubber bits that snap or perish.
- Never lay a hose across a driveway. Cars break hoses eventually.
- Use a Dramm water breaker to water all plants, not a hose nozzle.

Keep your hoses laid flat along garden and lawn edges so they don't kink.

A: A packet of 'O' rings.

B: Removing the broken 'O' ring.

C: Putting on the new 'O' ring.

D: You're back in business.

Necessities

You must have some soil wetting agent. For pots use Saturaid, for gardens use a liquid like Wettasoil.

You must keep Seasol on hand to get your plants growing. You could also use Amgrow Organic Harvest. Seaweed extracts are super tonics for plants. Not all seaweed products work satisfactorily. They must be smelly, gooey and brown to work.

You should get some budding tape. This plastic tape is much gentler on plants when you tie them to stakes, etc.

You need some cheap white plastic plant labels. When you do cuttings put: 'Azalea "Splendens" 12.11.08' or whatever is relevant so you know exactly when you took them and what they are.

A: Seasol can be applied mixed with water in a watering can or as a click-on hose attachment.

B: Budding tape is a simple and very gentle way to tie your plants to stakes.

A+B: Label your cuttings with white plastic labels. Cheap, easy, and really useful.

CHAPTER 2 *Getting it right*

Essential Tools (aka birthday or Christmas checklist)

Tools maketh the gardener

1. Spade
2. Shovel
3. Grass rake
4. Steel rake
5. Tomahawk or axe
6. Mattock
7. Bow saw
8. Pruning saw
9. Pair of secateurs
10. Pair of hedge trimmers (if you have a hedge)
11. Hammer
12. Large garden fork
13. Coarse broom
14. Garden trowel
15. Electric drill + masonry bits for holes in pots
16. Bench grinder
17. Spray gun (not too cheap)
18. Spirit level about 1m long
19. Stanley knife
20. Tape measure
21. Pencils for labelling
22. Stepladder

4. (right to left) A spade, coarse broom, large garden fork, grass rake, shovel and a steel rake.

6. A mattock and an axe

Secateurs (if your partner/kid really loves you, they include the pouch).

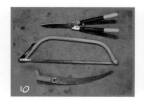

Hedge trimmers, a bow saw and a pruning saw.

A tape measure, Stanley knife, pencils and garden trowel.

Electric drill and masonry bits.

A bench grinder (a fantastic big birthday gift).

A spray gun.

A spirit level, 1m long, is ideal.

A stepladder.

CHAPTER 3

You could easily be doing something better with your time

Even the keenest gardener has a job or two that he or she hates doing. But the truly dedicated lazy gardener isn't keen on any gardening jobs at all. They could easily be doing something better with their time.

Worst job 1: Weeding

What's wrong with weeding

Almost everything. It never stops, the weeds always come back. Your fingernails fill up with dirt. It's boring. Your back aches afterwards. You could easily be doing something better with your time.

How to avoid weeding

- Mulch every square inch of soil in your garden. Apply mulches such as straw, lucerne, pea-straw, sugar cane mulch, forest fines or woodchip about 50mm deep everywhere. You can use inorganic mulches such as pebbles or gravel if you prefer, but they don't need to be applied as thickly.
- Plant something, it's more fun than weeding. Weeds are just plants which grow in bare patches, so cut down on the number of bare patches with either mulch or plants.
- Stop planting weeds! Some plants self-seed all over the place, and you end up with pests such as impatiens (busy lizzie), forget-me-nots, Californian poppies and cosmos popping up

Avoid weeds. Mulch with pea-straw.

Hardwood mulch.

Pebble mulch.

here, there and everywhere. So, stop planting them and you won't have to pull their babies out later on.

- Use sprays if you like. Glyphosate-based sprays such as Zero or Roundup make weeding easier, but just remember not to use these sprays anywhere within coo-ee of roses (they're super sensitive to these chemicals, even in nearby soil) and never ever use these sprays on a windy day, or the spray could drift onto something much prettier and more valuable than the weeds you're trying to kill.

Worst job 2: Watering gardens

What's wrong with watering gardens

These days, it's probably that you feel guilty. In the last couple of years there's been a campaign to make people feel guilty about watering their gardens, and I think it's working. Watering gardens can be a chore, but if you forget to do it your plants might die, especially the babies or the ones you transplanted last winter. Another really bad thing about watering gardens is that sometimes you want to do it, and you're not allowed. There's hardly any fun to be had watering gardens anymore. You could easily be doing something better with your time.

How to avoid watering gardens

Well, when I say 'watering gardens' I guess I mean standing there watering the garden with a hose in your hand. The perfect way to do it is *not* to stand there, and you can do that if you install a drip irrigation system. Spray irrigation systems have been regulated out of existence in many areas, but you can convert them over to drip irrigation. So ask an irrigation specialist for a conversion kit, and you're back in business.

- See 'how to avoid weeding' above, because mulching is also a beaut way to avoid weeding. **Big tip:** wait until it rains, and the soil gets well soaked, then apply your mulch. If it hasn't rained lately, don't mulch. Wait until it rains.

- Let your very thirsty plants die. Then replace them with something that isn't so thirsty.
- Every time you do water the garden, do it for 20–30 minutes, not five minutes. Now, this might seem like you're spending more time watering the garden, but in fact you're not. One good soaking can keep a garden going for a week or more. A five-minute sprinkle keeps plants happy for about a day, and you have to go out and water them again. Over a year, the 20–30 minute soaks actually save you time.

Worst job 3: Looking after lawns

What's wrong with looking after lawns

Lawns are the highest-maintenance things in any garden. They need mowing, weeding, edging, mowing, fertilising, watering, mowing and, quite often, more mowing. And I didn't even mention pest control! You could easily be doing something better with your time.

How to avoid caring for lawns

- You could just let your lawn go to wrack and ruin and grow long like a field of wheat, but divorces are messy and expensive, you'll miss the kids, so you'll need to come up with an alternative plan. Such as getting rid of the lawn altogether. That's right. No lawn at all is the ultimate no-mow lawn.
- Adopt a 'smaller-lawn' strategy. First of all get rid of all problem spots, such as the bare bits under shady trees where the lawn never grows. Just move the garden beds out a few more feet there, plant some shade-lovers such as clivias, and that's it. And maybe there's the bare patch where everyone takes a short-cut across the lawn. A simple paving job should fix that problem forever.
- Change the type of lawn grass if you have to. My best tip is to check out a soft leaf buffalo such as 'Sir Walter', which performs well in a very wide variety of climates, and it even handles dry spells and shady areas really well.
- Don't park your car on the lawn, even just to wash it. This will

Sir Walter buffalo grass is a hardy lawn option.

just compact the soil, making it impossible for grass to grow, and turn the lawn bare in the tyre tracks.

Worst job 4: Trimming plants

What's wrong with trimming plants

If your garden is a jungle, you probably gave up on trimming plants back a year or so ago. Just got too much for you in the end. Mind you, it can happen in a matter of weeks up in the tropics, especially in the wet season, but even in cooler parts of the country a wet, warm spell is all you need to make you really, really hate trimming back plants. You could easily be doing something better with your time.

How to avoid trimming plants

Don't plant climbers. There are so many rampant climbers planted in gardens that they probably make up half the workload of trimming back plants in most gardens. Get rid of rampant climbers such as wisteria and common jasmine (*Jasminum polyanthum*) in temperate areas, and in the tropics stay away entirely from gloriosa vine (*Gloriosa superba*) and blue trumpet vine (*Thunbergia*). If you really must have a climber for that spot in your garden, there are better behaved climbers available, such as star jasmine (*Trachelospermum jasminoides*), but even they will need some trimming occasionally.

- Choose the right-size plants for the spot you have in mind. If that 'hole' in your garden bed is 2m wide and you plant a 3m shrub there, you'll be trimming it back forever. And if that 4m wide shrub is planted 1.5m from the edge of the pathway, you have a job for life.

Worst job 5: Trimming flowers

What's wrong with trimming flowers

It seems like a good idea in theory. If you remove the finished flower heads from a flowering plant and stop it setting seed, the plant will then try to reproduce again by sending up even more flowers. Nothing wrong with that theory, because it's perfectly correct and the results are very pretty—but it's hard work. It takes much longer to do than you think, especially if you have lots of flowers. You could easily be doing something better with your time.

How to avoid trimming flowers

- Choose plants whose flowers last for ages—like salvias (sage), gazanias, alyssum, convolvulus, pelargoniums and catmint, for example. All of these just go on flowering and almost seem to thrive on neglect.

Gazania.

- Forget about flowers altogether and bring long-lasting colour into your garden via foliage. There are so many cordylines to choose from you can have almost any colour you want, and up in the tropics crotons are simply dazzling. Hardy flaxes (*Phormium* spp and cvs.) come in many different foliage colours, and easy-care bromeliads are ideal for growing in pots or even in the forks of trees.

Bromeliads are great all-rounders.

Worst job 6: Nursing pot plants

What's wrong with nursing pot plants

If the whole world is making you feel guilty about watering your garden, you'll probably need to go to confession each week if you're nursing pot plants. Especially in summer. They need constant watering then. And then every year or two you notice that the potting mix has slumped several inches and they all need repotting. You could easily be doing something better with your time.

How to avoid nursing pot plants

- Let your fuss-pots die. That's right, die. They're simply not worth it. Get something that's easier to care for. Succulents such as agaves, yuccas, echeverias, kalanchoes, aeoniums, etc. thrive in sunny spots. If you want flowers in your sunshiny pots, pelargoniums (ie. what everyone still calls geraniums) are the best bet and they come in a great range of colours, but the herb rosemary loves sunshine, flowers occasionally, produces leaves for cooking and its foliage smells divine when you brush past it. In a shady spot, clivias work very well and are tough. And if it's really shady, the aspidistra, the cast iron plant, is virtually unkillable and stays green and shiny all-year-round.

A: Pelargoniums.

B: Rosemary is a pretty plant that's great for cooking and barbecues.

C: Shade-loving clivias.

- While you're being ruthless and letting your fuss-pots die, be even more ruthless and cut down on the number of potted plants altogether.
- You can make life much easier for yourself by replacing all your little pots with just a few really big pots, tubs or planters. Remember, the smaller the pot, the faster its potting mix will dry out, so the bigger the pot the less often you'll have to water it.
- Don't skimp on the cost of potting mix. The better quality stuff does cost more, but it's better quality because it holds moisture better than the cheaper stuff. Look for mixes with added fertilisers and soil wetting agents.
- Finally, toss away the saucer under the pot. Go on, get rid of it altogether, and put your pots up on pot feet instead. Any potted plant which sits in a permanent pool of water, courtesy of a saucer, is slowly suffering and dying. It's drowning slowly, from the bottom up. Its roots are rotting away. Poor thing.

Worst job 7: Repairing water features

What's wrong with repairing water features

Everything. Leaky water features are genuine backyard tragedies.
Enough to make grown men weep. So much promise, sparkle, bubble
and delight when brand new, but two years later look what they've
become. It's so sad. If there's still any water left, it's green, slimy and
smells bad, and if there's no water left it just smells bad. It used to be
a status symbol, and now it's your own backyard nightmare to worry
about. You could easily be doing something better with your time.

How to avoid repairing water features

- You probably won't find this suggestion all that useful now, but if
  you never installed that water feature in the first place…oh, you
  don't want to hear that sort of stuff? Okay, I understand.
- How about just getting rid of the water feature altogether?
  They're a backyard disaster waiting to happen, and even at best
  they're a high maintenance item, even if you figure out how to
  keep everything leak free and clean.

Worst job 8:
Solving sick plant problems

What's wrong with solving sick plant problems

One day it's a happy looking plant and then a week later its leaves
are yellow and it's on the way out. Nothing extraordinary happened
in the week in-between—no heatwaves, blizzards or plagues of
locusts, and yet your backyard hospital has another patient in the
plant ward. It wouldn't be so bad if you knew what the problem was,
and now you'll have to spend time trying to diagnose what's wrong
before you can even try to fix it. You could easily be doing something
better with your time.

How to avoid sick plant problems

- Save money—get rid of the plant and buy something else. It probably was planted in the wrong spot to start with. Here's how you save money by buying another plant. Many people will spend $30 on chemical sprays, plant foods and tonics trying to save their sick $9 plant. Instead, be ruthless, spend $9 on another more suitable plant for the spot and you've saved $21.

- So try planting something else there, but this time round, talk to the people at the garden centre about the vacant spot you have, and look for a plant that matches the spot perfectly. First of all, measure up the vacant spot to get the plant size right. Then figure out how many hours of sunshine it gets each day in summer, and then in winter. Check out the soil type (ie, sandy, loam or clay) and whether the soil there is usually dry, wet or roughly in-between. With this info, you should be able to find a likely candidate.

- Go for a wander around your neighbourhood and look for healthy, similar-sized plants growing in the same sort of spot where your sick plant failed to do well in. Ask the owner the name of that plant (who knows, they might even give you a cutting or two) and have a go at growing that local success story in your own backyard.

Worst job 9: Climbing ladders
What's wrong with climbing ladders

It's those official accident statistics from the hospitals that worry old ladder climbers. Men falling off ladders. Lots of them do it. And the older they get, the more of them fall off, it seems. Once they get past 50, the statistics climb as rapidly as the older Aussies tumble. So, the less we all have to climb ladders the better. But when an outdoor light fitting goes on the blink, gutters fill up with leaves, leaks mysteriously appear in the roof, then you're back up on that rotten ladder again. You could easily be doing something better with your time.

How to avoid climbing ladders
- Get someone younger and fitter to do the job for you if you've passed 50 years of age. There's no shame involved. As you get older your sense of balance loses its edge. If you don't feel as confident up on the ladder as you used to, that's the cue for you to get your son, nephew, neighbour's boy or whoever you can find to help you out.
- Don't work alone on a ladder, or let anyone helping out work alone on a ladder. Have someone there holding the ladder for you. And pay full attention to all ladder safety basics. Make sure the ladder's feet are on solid ground; have the ladder set back from the house/guttering or whatever it's leaning on so the set-back is around one-quarter of the height of the structure it's leaning on; set up the ladder so there's at least 1m of ladder above the structure it's leaning on.
- If outdoor light-fittings are failing regularly, look into replacing them with long-life globes that rarely, if ever, fail. The new generation of LED outdoor lights is getting much better, and they hold the promise that you might never have to touch them again. The only drawback with them is that they are still quite expensive, but they are getting cheaper, and brighter. If you can't afford them, even a good old Portaflood light, which is cheap as chips, should last for years without needing replacement.

Worst job 10: Feeding plants

What's wrong with feeding plants

Most people don't actually dislike feeding plants, it's more that they simply forget to do it. Perhaps what they don't like is the fact they feel guilty when their plants look crook, because they know that if they remembered to feed them they might be still alive. Feeling guilty–you could easily be doing something better with your time!

Feeding plants the lazy way

This is so easy. Just use slow-release fertilisers (such as Osmocote). These come in all sorts of formulations for everything from fruit trees through to natives, pot plants, indoor plants, bonsai, roses and lots more. You only need to apply them once or twice a year, it only takes a few minutes each time, and that's it! All you have to do is remember to do it next year…

Right: For lazy plant feeding, use slow-release fertilisers such as Osmocote.

CHAPTER 4
The Duck's Nuts

*W*e all want our place to be the best on earth. The Acme, Nonpareil, The Bees Knees or, in Australian: the Duck's Nuts (occasionally the Duck's Guts).

So here follows the down-to-earth guide to a backyard that works. The front yard is just a lump of blancmange for the rubbernecks that stagger past. The backyard is about us, who we are, what we need.

First, buy a cheap compass. I have a cheap keyring compass that I bought from the Australian Geographic store. It's in my pocket all the time. North is where most of the sun comes from. A garden that faces north—ie. is open to the north—is sunny. One that faces south is shady. One that faces east gets morning sun (gentle, but causes frost damage in cooler areas) and one that faces west gets arvo sun, which can be too strong for some plants, but will be very kind to tropical plants like avocados, mangos and frangipanis.

Need no.1

No house should ever end. In a useful home, the home gradually transforms itself into the outdoors. Ideally, the whole back of the house has concertina doors so it all opens up. Parties spill out onto the patio and kids spill into the living room. The end result of this is that the home *includes* all of the backyard. It becomes bloody huge.

It's a great idea to use the same tiles or pavers inside in the living room and outside on the patio. On the patio should be some seriously comfortable chairs, a huge table, a barbeque and loads of potted herbs and perhaps vegies and strawberries.

You lean across from your chair and snatch a fistful of coriander for your barbequed prawns. Or perhaps a few strawberries for your champagne. You chuck them, still wriggling, into your glass.

Over the top of the table is a Solarspan roof. Fully insulated, it cuts out the heat of summer. It starts from above the guttering and slopes upwards into the backyard.

This way the rain goes back into the gutter and the Solarspan roof is high and lets in lots of light. Solarspan is industrial refrigerator material, but they now do a roofing profile on top and a white Colorbond underneath with insulation in between.

Concertina doors allow
the house to spill out
into the backyard.

Solarspan cross section:
Roofing profile on top and white
Colorbond underneath, with
insulation in between.

If you want the Duck's Nuts, do not put in a pergola. Pergolas look okay but they add nothing practical to your house. A decent, God-fearing roof will provide superb protection from both sun and rain. Then the house really does spill out into the garden. And you know what? You can put comfy furniture under a rain-proof roof: not just painful wooden stuff without cushions.

Need no.2

Plan out what you will build or get when you have the dough. A swimming pool, a humungous shed or pavilion, a bigger garage, a vegie garden, a compost area, a fish pond, a kids' play area or whatever. Plan out all of those needs now and maybe do a rough sketch of what might go where.

- Swimming pools need to be near the house in a line of sight from the kitchen and/or living room. Just in case one of the kids topples into the pool. The pool should be in full sun and not too close to leaf-dropping trees. The worst are jacarandas, silky-oaks, wattles and gum trees. The best are palms and deciduous trees (the leaves all drop in two to three weeks and that's it–not all year like gum trees). You also need to leave truck access for the pool if you can't build it for a year or two.

- A pavilion is a great idea. This is for wet days' play for the kids, adult parties, music practice, etc. The refrigerator panels already mentioned are excellent for this. These panels are easily carried in by two people.
- Garages are so important. Use them as work sheds, play areas on wet days, painting areas and table tennis zones. A roller door front *and* back is a good idea for machinery access to the backyard.
- The vegie garden and compost area should be up the back of the yard in full sun.
- Fish ponds stay cleaner out of full sun as sun causes algae. Fish ponds, like swimming pools, are best near the house for safety reasons.
- Kids' play areas can be centrally located in the yard and should have some hidey-holes where kids can be secretive.

Need no.3

Patience. If you have just bought the place, wait at least a year before you chop anything out. Wait for the seasons to come and go. For the maples to colour in autumn or the bulbs to appear in spring. Don't get territorial and chop out the ugly tree out the front. It may turn into a spectacular beauty in a few weeks. Spend a year doing the inside.

Need no.4

Go for a walk: Walk hither and yon. Look at what grows well and what doesn't. If you like something, pop in to the place and knock on the door. Tell them how nice their place is and how you love the shrub or tree or groundcover you have seen. Ask them what it is. If they don't know, ask if you can take a small piece of it to the local nursery for identification. Ask the locals what grows well in the area. Ask them about the soils and rainfall. This could save you thousands of dollars. Local knowledge is *king*.

Need no.5

Garden rooms: Set out a series of outdoor rooms for entertaining, for footy and cricket, for clothes drying or whatever. These areas can be divided by some low shrubs, latticework or just a spill-over of plants from a garden bed. But you do need defined areas to make a garden work.

Need no.6

Paths: Once a few plants are in, it's time to think about paths. Just think, don't do anything. Wait for the goat-tracks to form. Wait until the wear marks of the tide of humanity in your backyard appear. This is where the paths should go. So often people put in paths where they look good, so for the next 50 years people take a short-cut across the lawn. Damn!

Defined areas or garden rooms really make a garden the Duck's Nuts.

Need no.7

Dirt: Don't buy soil. Most soil sold in Australia is not very good. This is especially true in Sydney and Brisbane. Buy organic matter and very coarse sand. The organic matter can be composted green waste plus animal manures. Always remember that your site soil, the soil on your block, is the best soil you can get. Just improve it as necessary with organic matter and sand.

    If you have to buy soil, contact a swimming pool company to see if they might deliver a truckload of real excavated soil from a local garden. Clay is fine, just get over your hangups. Clay soils are good…Oh, all right, let's look at soils.

Most backyards are full of the best soil you can get. To make them even better, dig in some organic matter and coarse sand.

A (sandy soil): If your snake cracks as soon as you bend it, it's a sandy soil.

B (loam): If your snake makes a semi-circle, then cracks, it's a loam.

C (clay): If it forms a perfect circle, it's a clay soil.

You need to know what sort of soil you have, so grab about a golfball-sized lump and wet it a bit. The idea is to get it like plasticine so that you can roll it into a snake. Next, try to bend the snake into a circle. If it cracks as soon as you bend it, this is a sandy soil. If it bends about half way to a circle, then cracks, it's a loam. If it forms a perfect circle like plasticine, it is a clay soil.

- **Sandy soils:** Add bulk compost from your local landscape supplier. Lay a 10cm (4in) layer of mulch on top of the soil and fork it well in. You can use some of the compost as a surface mulch too.

- **Loams:** Also dig in some compost as above.

- **Clay soils:** Also dig in some compost as above, but add about a handful of gypsum or some clay breaker before you dig it all over. It is always a good idea to create raised beds in clay soils. Raise them up, just by heaping, about 30–50cm (12–20in) above the surrounding ground.

- **Un-dirt:** Crushed sandstone is far better for native plants than bought soil. Most crushed rock (except limestone) is better for natives than purchased soil. Just add some organic matter.

Using crushed rock

Here, crushed rock is laid on top of a large rock ledge. No soil was there. The crushed sandstone was laid about 20cm (8in) deep for the paths and from 60cm (24in) to 1.5m (5ft) high in the raised garden beds. Then a 10cm (4in) layer of bulk composted humus was spread on top of the sandstone.

Next, the grevilleas and other plants were planted. In the process, some of the humus was mixed with the crushed sandstone in and around the planting holes. Lastly, the whole area was mulched with a 7.5cm (3in) layer of leaf litter.

A: A handful of crushed sandstone.

B: The crushed sandstone is in place, the paths are formed and the capping of humus is on top. Note the large lumps of rock—this is okay.

C: The plants are now planted and the leaf mulch is on top of the humus and crushed sandstone.

D: The garden after eight months.

E (right): The garden after two-and-a-half years.

Need no.8

The old 'put-and-look' method: If you can't be bothered drawing up a design of your garden, place plants here and there and stand back and look. Move them until they look good. Read the labels too and try to envisage the final height of each plant. Once you are satisfied, plant them.

If you can't be bothered drawing a design, do the put-and-look. Place your plants, in their pots, around the garden, until you are happy with their position, then plant away.
Tip: Check the labels to see how tall they grow.

Need no.9

Bloody weeds: Spread mulch 35mm deep. Use leaf litter, wood chip, pea straw, spoiled lucerne hay or compost. Pinebark is a little tough on the soil unless it is composted first (before you buy it). And plant lots of shrubs and groundcovers. Never leave any bare areas for weeds to grow. Chock it up. But don't plant things around roses or citrus–they don't like it. No grass around the citrus either–keep it at least 2m from the trunk. The older books say to put mulch on 75 to 100mm thick. New research says far less–35mm.

Fill all these needs and you will have little work to do. The garden will largely just bubble along. Go to the beach or the footy or the movies. Better still, stay at home and enjoy fresh food and lots of satisfaction as the plants grow.

Spread mulch 35mm deep. Spoilt lucerne makes a great mulch.

CHAPTER 5
Fantasies

*A*ll great gardens are works of fantasy, and most of the greatest gardens exist in ordinary streets in ordinary suburbs. It's just that these great gardens, great for their humanity, don't feature in gardening books.

As a young nurseryman, I met a bloke who bought some ferns from the nursery. He said he had a palm garden and that I should pop in and see it. I'd never heard of a palm garden in Sydney (it was the early '70s) so I popped in. He had hundreds and hundreds of dirty great big palms. This was a quarter-acre block and it looked like a scene from a Tarzan movie. In the middle of it was a jungle pool for swimming in. There were overhanging tropical vines, the whole shebang.

So, my curiosity raised, I asked, 'What do you use it for?' He had no lawn, no neat shrubs, just a quarter acre of steaming sensuality. 'Well it's just my garden,' he said.

'Bulldust,' I thought. 'Do you and the missus use it for fun?' I asked. 'Well, sort of,' he said.

Getting more curious, I asked, 'Do you and the missus have Tarzan and Jane costumes and do the full jungle thing?' 'Yeah, it's saved our marriage–really re-kindled the flame.'

In that instant, I realised that all of my studies were wasted. Every garden book I read was a mistake. Gardens were about people, not plants, pots and rocks. How could I have been so stupid?

I still imagine him beating his chest, letting out a blood-curdling cry as he sweeps his Jane off her feet and she melts into his arms. Now that's gardening!

Maybe your dream is to create a Hobbiton bunker for the kids. We did this once on *Backyard Blitz*. I dreamed up an underground bunker made out of a concrete water tank. This was sunken into the ground and a lid was fitted about 30cm (12in) above the tank so the kids could spy on everyone else. We put soil on top of the lid and fitted a periscope through all of it and electronic CCTV cameras as well. They could observe the whole neighbourhood. There were bike tracks, a girls' castle and lots of other things. Every kid for miles around descended on the place and months later it was still a smash hit.

A kid's dream: Their own backyard bunker.

Children deserve their own land rights—backyard spaces where they can live out their fantasies, explore nature, get dirty, build things—secret areas that belong to them, like this fantastic backyard in Brisbane.

Parents these days spend a fortune on their kids' formal education, but out in the backyard their informal education is too often neglected. As a kid, I learnt my first lessons about keeping pets (mice) out in the backyard. I built my first road there (out of mud, for my Matchbox cars), and I created my own secret world in those fascinating, spidery 'caves' under our house. As a kid I took my backyard land rights for granted. Whole sections of our backyard were mine. Everyone knew that.

Too many kids these days are missing out on their backyard land rights, and when this happens there's a huge chunk missing from their development—the private play time that helps shape their imagination. They need places to explore, private zones to live out their fantasies and find out about life for themselves. They also need opportunities to see nature in action: birds building nests and squabbling over food, spiders weaving webs, ladybirds and praying mantises at work, seeds sprouting and flowers blooming. They'll see their pets showing traces of the wild animal lurking within (eg. puss hunting the birds). Yes, they'll get dirty, but that won't do them any harm. In fact, being outdoors and getting a bit grubby will probably help to build up their immune system and make them more robust and healthy in the long run.

The Bunker

Top of the list for a private space for kids would have to be a cubby house. Any good cubby house soon becomes a club house, and lots of parents will probably never learn (well, not until years later) what the secret club in the cubby house was really all about.

In this Brisbane backyard pictured here, we put all these ideas into practice—private zones for the kids, cubby houses, fantasy zones, places for them to explore.

As I said, to create the wonderful kids' bunker, complete with periscope, we buried a concrete tank in the ground and put a roof on it. Then we added walkie-talkies, low-voltage lights, closed circuit TV and the amazing periscope. The kids can stay hidden in the bunker and secretly spy on the house or yard. With the walkie-talkies they can send messages to each other. In the bunker, their secret society can meet.

We added plants for camouflage to help make the bunker private, and if you want to do the same thing, just remember the water-drainage issues. The ideal set-up would be on a sloping block, building the bunker half-in and half-out of the ground. On flat ground, you'll need to provide drainage from the bottom of the bunker.

A: The amazing periscope!

B: The kids love using the walkie-talkies and binoculars for their secret spy games.

Something for everyone: A hidden bunker, a bike path and a pretty garden.

Creating a magical fairy garden became my obsession.

The Fairy Garden

While on the kids' theme, we also did a very moving story about Morgyn, a 2-year-old girl (now 5) who had cancer. She was undergoing treatment and was miserable. She didn't even want to get out of bed some mornings. Loved fairies though, so I thought we could build her a fairy garden. I'd never seen one, other than a garden with a few little fairy statues instead of gnomes.

This became an obsession with me and it took months to organise. We had a normal garden design drawn up, then I set to work to turn it into a fairy village. My crazy ideas included a hollow-log house with doors, windows and a roof—but full of fairies and furniture and all the comforts of a fairy home. There were fairy lights everywhere, more fairies dancing on a moss garden, more fairies in trees, fairies hidden everywhere.

We added glitter to everything—wet paint, soil, pathways, etc. Nothing succeeds like excess. The colours of Morgyn's fairy tea house (full size) matched the Brachyscome 'Mauve Delight' and other plants which surrounded it. We also put fairy stuff all through Morgyn's bedroom, which looked out onto the garden. She was totally transformed by the garden—rising at dawn each day, excited to go into the garden. Her parents said the garden changed her life.

This wonderful fairy garden is everything imaginative little girls could wish for. And the great thing about it is that the average home handyperson could do a pretty good copy of it in any backyard. The tea house is easy enough to build, and all the magical fairy accessories which give it so much charm can be bought at specialist fairy shops.

A: The looks on the imagination-filled faces of children make buiding a fairy garden so worthwhile.

B: Fairies placed throughout the garden added a magical touch.

The Tea House

The tea house isn't hard to build if you're handy with a saw, hammer and a paintbrush. Its frame is pink-primed treated pine (65mm x 45mm). This timber is a bit more expensive, but it's worth using if you want a good result that lasts outdoors. Pink-primed timbers are straight and true, and make it much easier to get everything to line up perfectly.

The floor for the tea house is hardwood decking boards, and the walls and roof are 12mm plywood. We attached thatching to the plywood to give the roof that old-world cottage-in-the-forest look, but timber shingles would look cute on the roof too, as would the right paint job.

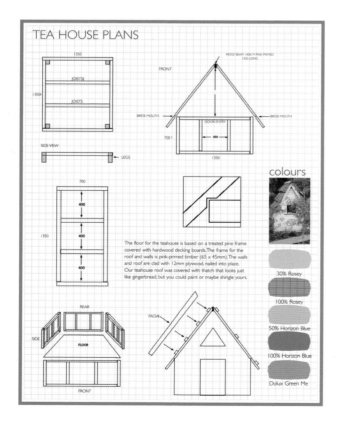

Left: The fairy tea house plans.

Right: The magical fairy tea house

Colour clues

As for paints, it was easy to choose the main colour–pink, please! But here's a good trick for colour-coordinating with paints: start with a darker colour and change its tint by mixing it with a white paint.

Our pink paint is Dulux 'Rosey'. When used at full-strength it's a dark pink. For our tea house we mixed one part 'Rosey' with three parts white to get the pretty, light 'little-girl' pink we were after. Then we used 'Rosey' at full strength for the painted mushrooms on the walls of the tea house, and the blend of hues is superb. Out in the garden we kept the pink theme going with our choice of pink salvias, excellent long-lasting, easy-care flowers.

We did the same thing with our blue paints. We started off with a dark blue, Dulux 'Horizon Blue', and mixed this 50:50 with white paint to create our light blue. Out in the garden, blue salvias are a perfect match for the full-strength 'Horizon Blue'. On the tea house, you can see the light blue on the window frames and eaves, and the dark blue in the flowers on the walls.

And if you're wondering what the light green colour is on the details for the tea house walls, that's Dulux 'Green Me'.

Fairy Pink

Pink salvia

We mixed one part of Dulux 'Rosey' (above right) with three parts of white to create the pink for the tea house.

Pretty Blues

Blue Salvia

We used one part Dulux 'Horizon Blue' (above right) with one part of white to colour the tea house trims.

Magically Red

Canna lily

The hot tones of the canna lily combine with the fibreglass mushrooms from Animation and Display in Melbourne.

Pink salvia, blue salvia and canna lily complemented the colours of the tea house.

Fairy's House

Normally, that enchanted tea house would be the 'piece de resistance' of any little girl's fairy garden, but we all fell in love with the special little fairy house we added nearby. This is the place where the fairies live, and you can peek inside the windows and see them there, eating their fairy bread and nibbling on fairy cakes.

A country property provided the perfect hollow log for our fairy house. Then we used a jigsaw to cut out the windows and doors. Into the glitter-painted interiors—which really do sparkle—we then added little fairy figurines, plus tiny pieces of furniture including beds and rocking chairs (from the Hocus Pocus Fairy Shop in Bondi Junction, Sydney). Some thatching attached to a plywood pyramid, set on top

A: The fairies live in the enchanted log house.

B: If you are very quiet you can peek through the windows and see the fairies inside.

C: At night, the fairy log becomes even more magical.

of the log, creates the perfect conical roof, and hand-made 'window frames' of 10mm quad set over Perspex windows almost completes the scene. Almost? Well, you need lights on at night for the perfect fairy's home, don't you? Of course, so we set up some low-voltage lights inside the log, which we can switch on at night to show that the fairies are at home and snug in bed.

Everyone who sees this fairy's home is delighted by it. It's the wonderful little miniature world you see when you peer inside the windows that provide the magical delight. And at night, when the lights are on and the glitter paint sparkles, it's just so easy for little girls to believe that fairies are real!

Play zones

Setting up a child's swing in a fairy woodland needed a bit of extra panache so it didn't look out of place, so we decided on a 'flower bower' swing. Our bower is actually a 60mm curved, galvanised pipe concreted into place and garlanded with artificial flowers. (You could try attaching a climber to the swing frame, but that would need a fair bit of maintenance and clipping, and we wanted the swing to be concealed from the day it was built.)

Attached to this sturdy frame is a rubber swing seat (which conforms to Australian Standards, a design and safety assurance rating that parents should make sure comes with any children's swing equipment they buy). A pink-rimmed sandpit under the swing says this is where the fairy princesses come to play and talk.

A great spot for a swing, with a sandpit underneath for a soft landing.

A: Cheerful mushrooms brighten up the garden and give the fairies something to dance around.

B: The red mushrooms are made from fibreglass.

Magical garden

Those cheerful mushrooms in the garden are made from fibreglass, so they're light and safe should they topple over (the concrete ones could hurt a child, so take care to make sure they are solidly mounted if you use them). Our mushrooms came from Animation and Display in Melbourne. Planted around the mushrooms in our magical garden is a classic cottagey blend of flowers such as salvias and foxgloves, as well as canna lilies, woodland grasses and flowering climbers.

At night, the whole garden comes alive when the fairy lights, with their snowdrop and ladybird lanterns, are switched on.

Design details

Even though we had lots of fun building the fairy's house and the tea house, setting up the swing, planting out the garden, running out the fairy lights, adding the mushrooms and playing with paints, the best fun by far with this garden was seeing the reaction on the little girls' faces when they discovered 'real' fairies in their garden.

Around Australia there's a remarkably good array of shops specialising in fairy-themed accessories, and online there are even more. You can get carried away with all the fairy shopping—we did! When we found the beautiful bronze and fibreglass fairies online at www.efairies.com we gulped a bit when we saw the prices ranging

A: A fairy from efairies.com.

B: These ladybird lights are from Living Ideas Imports.

from $60 to $200, but we just had to have some! And like us, you might find it hard to resist the lovely ladybird garden lights. But when you see the looks on those imagination-filled faces of the children, it's worth every cent and all the effort creating it.

For the blokes

We did a backyard makeover for the blokes in Jimboomba, Queensland. This was our first big pavilion. Using a then-new material called Solarspan (an industrial refrigeration panelling) we constructed an outdoor room measuring 6m x 10m. It included a flat-screen TV, an oven, stoves, a two-door fridge, a huge dining table and chairs, sinks, lights…the lot. It also featured a concertina-door front. Remember that the whole structure is made of refrigerator panelling (Solarspan), which is insulated against both heat and cold.

This pavilion is the ultimate in outdoor entertaining because everything is indoors–except you're out in the backyard. Makes perfect sense to me.

We decided to build this ultimate entertainer's garden and put the works into it: ultra-cool walls and ceilings that beat summer's heat; gourmet chef's kitchen complete with barbecue, sink, fridge and ice-maker; sliding doors that open up the area to the outdoors on those perfect balmy days; plasma screen TV to watch the footy and the cricket; big table with comfy chairs to handle a crowd.

There's no roughing it out here. No balancing a plate on your lap. No winter chills. No summer sunburn. It's civilised, very civilised. The perfect place to be lazy, a completely self-sufficient outdoor entertaining area.

Relaxing space

A pavilion is a world apart in backyard comfort. It has a concrete slab underneath, plus special walls and roofing, as well as power and plumbing. And it also has plenty of space.

In fact, for this pavilion we found the perfect table first, then came

A: The self-contained pavilion is a welcome addition to any garden.

B: One for the blokes.

C: Dishwasher and sink.

A: And an icemaker
in the fridge!

B: The area in front of
the pavilion is the perfect
place for kids to play.

C: The ultimate
entertainer's pavilion.

up with our pavilion dimensions second. Our perfect table is a big one (2.5m x 1m) and it seats 10 comfortably. But it's also second-hand, super solid and just a tiny bit knocked around (they called it 'patina' at the second-hand furniture store, but a tiny bit knocked around is closer to the mark). No-one will ever bother if you accidentally spill something on this table, or even scratch it. It's a table everyone can feel relaxed around. The chairs are also big, solid and comfy real leather chairs. Neither the table nor chairs are pieces of outdoor furniture. They're indoor furniture items, and they're totally at home in our civilised pavilion.

We allowed a 1.2m space around the table but extra space (1.8m) at the back to allow access to the fridge and sinks without irritating those seated nearby. The pavilion itself is 5.67m long and 4.67m deep. The paved area extending 4m out in front of the pavilion lets you move the table outdoors on those lovely, warm spring and autumn days.

Special walls

Our structure is closed in on three sides, and also roofed, with Solarspan. This is the same material used to build refrigerated rooms, and its thermal insulation properties are brilliant. It's beautifully cool inside the pavilion on the hottest summer day, and warm as toast in winter. The other, fourth wall, that faces the rest of the garden, is a set of cedar bi-fold doors. On perfect days you open them up and it's outdoor living at its finest. On less than perfect days, you're laughing. You're inside the perfect pavilion.

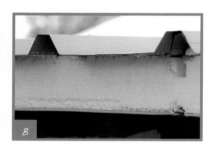

A: *The insulated Solarspan walls.*

B: *The Solarspan roof.*

Bibs and bobs

We included all the bibs and bobs you'd expect with a perfect pavilion. The ceiling has downlights, the benches have overhead cupboards and the stove has an exhaust fan. There's a two-door fridge and there's a plasma TV on the wall. In cooler southern climates you might want to fit strip heaters on the walls or hang them from the ceiling.

The owner said later that he was really upset that he had bought State of Origin tickets earlier on as he would *much* rather have watched the footy in his outdoor room.

A: All the best bibs and bobs were put in the pavilion.

B: The blokes have never been happier.

The design I'm most proud of is the French Provincial makeover. It looks like an old-fashioned garden from the French countryside, but we built it just a few years ago in a suburb of Sydney.

French provincial garden

The design I'm most proud of was our French provincial makeover on *Burke's Backyard*. It is another classic example of a garden designed around the family. The house was owned by a lady who loved the French provincial look: old paintings of chooks and pigs on the walls, wooden ladders on the kitchen ceiling from which the saucepans hang, French windows and, of course, French doors. The moment I saw inside the house I knew exactly what the garden should be: that is, her indoor ideas used outside.

My thoughts were of a French provincial garden—the sort of practical, but old-fashioned garden that you could stumble on in the French countryside.

Perhaps a little neglected, a bit ramshackle, with an old barn still standing and dominating the view. I found a photo of just such an old barn in France and I built up a series of photos of French roof tiles, old, neglected gardens and details from French outdoor restaurants as inspiration.

All of our team scoured junk shops, old farms and rural old wares shops. We located second-hand timber, second-hand chook wire and so much more.

For the design, I placed the old barn smack dab in the middle of the view from the house. It was to become a chook shed, but it can also be a kids' cubby house or a glorious garden shed.

It's the detailing of this garden that makes all the difference. We could have put a slab of galvo on the chook shed roof–most people do. But we went to the trouble to source second-hand roofing tiles made in Marseilles–authentic French provincial–and don't they make a difference! Even the big old door hinges on the chook shed, found at a demolition yard, look the part. And the rusted tin rooster standing on top of the chook shed truly is a 'piece de resistance'.

A: This gorgeous photo was my inspiration: it is a real barn in France. Our 'copy' is almost identical.

B: We sourced second-hand roofing tiles that were actually made in Marseilles, France.

C + D: I built up a series of other photos of neglected French gardens and other ideas as further inspiration.

A: The big old rusted hinges that we put on the chook shed were found at a demolition yard and look perfect.

B: The rusted rooster is truly a 'piece de resistance'.

C: We added many country-style touches such as this charming ladies' pushbike which became home to potted geraniums and succulents.

D: New farmyard items such as this pump were painted with Porter's 'Instant Rust' to make them look like ancient relics.

While the barn brought out the best in all of us, all around the garden there are authentic old country-style touches, such as the charming ladies' pushbike that's home to some potted succulents and geraniums, and the rack of old-style garden tools hanging from nails on the shed wall. The potting bench area is completely new yet looks like it has been there since Grandma was a girl.

And we happily resorted to some improvising when we couldn't find the 'authentic' old items. For example, we glued small strips of wood onto the existing sliding aluminium garage window to create the look of French windows. In other areas, we used 'Instant Rust' by Porter's Paints to turn new farmyard items into ancient rustic survivors which look like they've been there for generations.

A: Small strips of wood were glued onto an existing aluminium garage window, and flanked with second-hand shutters to create the look of real French windows.

B: The potting bench area is new, yet looks like it's been around since Grandma was a girl.

Meadows

French countryside wouldn't look right without meadows of flowers, so that's what we created in front of the barn. Two beds edged with wicker were planted out with cottage garden favourites such as gaura, dietes, various daisies (seaside, marguerite and angel), pineapple sage, *Salvia* 'Navajo Bright Red' and *Hemerocallis* 'Stella Bella'.

But as you reach the chook fence around the barn, the garden changes to nasturtiums and pumpkins that scramble up the wire.

A: Two meadow-like flower beds were edged with wicker and planted out with gorgeous, blousy, garden favourites.

B: Gaura.

C: Salvia 'Navajo Bright Red'.

A: The newly planted potager (French kitchen) garden.

B: The second hand bricks in the potager garden were laid in a classic basket-weave pattern.

C: The potager garden yields herbs and vegetables all year.

Kitchen garden

Around the side of the chook shed, near the back fence, we established a new Potager garden (ie. a French kitchen garden), whose beds are separated by rustic-looking paving of second-hand common bricks, laid in a classic basket-weave pattern. Again, it's the lovely attention to detail—the crusty old bricks, the ancient wire gate (found at a junk shop), the gap-toothed paling fence around the area—which gives it its charm. And it's functional, too. We planted chillies, tomatoes, lettuce, spinach, pumpkins and eggplant, as well as a good variety of herbs, including parsley, sage, basil, oregano, and, naturally enough for this French country garden, some French tarragon. I can't tell you how much fun we had putting all of our bric-a-brac together in this project.

Areas underfoot

The mixture of paved surfaces combines well. In addition to the old-style brick paving around the kitchen garden, the paths leading from the house out to the chook shed are of decomposed granite. This is a beautiful light gold-coloured surface, and it's very hard wearing and easy care. But it's how we laid it that makes all the difference. We lined the pathways with H4 treated pine edging (ie, rated for in-ground use) then laid down 50mm of road-base and compacted that. Then we laid a 50mm layer of decomposed granite, which was mixed with cement at a ratio of 8:1. We then lightly hosed down the decomposed granite to set the cement and also bring the gold colour to the surface.

For the short hop from the gate to the chook shed door, we laid some sandstone flagging, to make it clean underfoot for someone dashing from the house to the chook shed to fetch some breakfast eggs from the verrrrry French Faverolle chooks contentedly clucking inside.

And finally, the petanque lawns were turfed with 'Sir Walter' soft leaf buffalo, but only after we sloped the ground away from the house, to improve drainage (which had been a serious problem in the past). Petanque is French boules where you lob metal bowls to be nearest the jack. We presented Sarah with a petanque set, but really the lawn was for the kids.

The garden paths are made from decomposed granite mixed with cement at a ratio of 8:1.

A: The golden colour of the decomposed granite is tres magnifique!

B: French Faverolle chooks.

Lemony scents

We planted one of the most underrated native trees, the lemon-scented myrtle (*Backhousia citriodora*) on either side of the chook shed, and we also added a lemon tree inside the run. The foliage of the lemon-scented myrtle is so fragrant it's lovely to be pottering around feeding the chooks, and back in the kitchen you can use the lemon myrtle leaves in cooking.

Another world

Now, when she stands at the back door or, better still, at her French doors and looks out at her backyard, Sarah sees the complete country-style fantasy before her. And it's a completely natural transition from her beautiful French country-style home out into her little patch of fantasy farmyard. It's the kind of

A perfect patch of fantasy farmyard.

Star Jasmine colonises an old spade we placed in the garden.

garden she has always dreamed of and which will give her years of pleasure, and in anyone's eyes that makes it the perfect makeover.

Get the look

By now, you must be aware of the trickery, deceit and outright dishonesty of all great gardens. They make some boring bit of inner-city backyard look like an endless tropical rainforest. Or a banal suburban yard look like a fairyland. Or a nothing backyard look like provincial France. It's all fake and it's all easy.

Rainforest look: Just shove it altogether—Bangalow palms, New Zealand flax, New Zealand cordyline, ginger plants, bird's nest ferns, golden cane palms, rhapis palms, *Cordyline rubra*, *Cordyline fruticosa*, crinums, any ferns at all, anything with huge glossy leaves, anything with strap like leaves (even clivias). Tall stuff at the back, small at the front. Just check at the local nursery that all of the plants grow in your area. The main tip here is to pack lots of dense plants in front of the fences so that you can't see them.

Snowforests: You can grow a 'tropical rainforest' in Hobart or Launceston. There are superb palm trees like the Windmill palm, *Trachycarpus fortunei*, or even a stunning silver-leafed form of the Mediterranean Fan Palm, *Chamaerops humilis v. cerifera*: both together tolerate snow and both will grow in Canberra too. Remember that New Zealand cordylines (*Cordyline australis*) and New Zealand flaxes (*Phormium tenax*) also will tolerate miserably

Above and left: Dennis Hundschiedt's amazing tropical rainforest garden is pure fantasy created on an average-sized Brisbane house block.

cold conditions (that's called New Zealand weather). *Acanthus mollis* has huge, glossy maple-like leaves, plus superb purple and white flowers on 75cm (30in) tall stems–and it loves the cold. The only problem with growing a rainforest in Tassie is that the range of plants sold there in nurseries is not great. You may need to import the plants yourself–and this could involve quarantine.

All 'rainforest' type gardens have lots of organic matter: compost, leaf and woodchip mulches and manures.

Serenity

We can't avoid it any longer: Serenity. This really is the most important bit of any garden. A nice place to stick your bottom while you switch off. But how do you build serenity? Here follows the Kerrigan family's dead-set guide to Serenity:

1. **Enclosure:** We all want to be hugged. We are programmed to prefer certain special configurations–most of us feel uncomfortable in a wide open space if we are alone. In a garden you need trees to form the walls and ceiling of outdoor rooms. Effective outdoor rooms are just a little bigger than the rooms in your house: 5m x 5m is cosy but 10m x 10m is a bit big. Build smaller spaces that hug or embrace you as you sit there.

2. **Views:** We all like to peer at people and things. The people on the Sydney ferries and the ferries themselves are known as rubbernecks–in reference to the extreme efforts to see into everyone's backyards and lives. An ideal view is a line of sight between two objects. So a distant view between two trees in the foreground. You get a peek at the view. (A plunging neckline is similar: it draws the eye.) In the background you may wish to place a statue, potted plant or specimen plant as the view with a foreground of two shrubs or two lines of shrubs: NEVER

set up a line of sight between two formal rows of plants without an object at the end. It's awful to draw the eye to a blank space. That's why us blokes don't wear plunging necklines.

A potted plant or statue creates a focal point.

3. **Ponds:** Sitting beside a pond watching the goldfish glide by is superbly relaxing. Watching the fish sail under a lily-pad as they effortlessly slide through the water is just sheer serenity. So stick in a pond. No matter what, stick a butyl liner under all home-made pools. Every pond leaks and it can drive you nuts. Butyl rubber liners stop the leaks. They cost money, but you need them.

4. **Green:** Somehow green whispers sweet nothings to your psyche. Soft green ferns, velvety green moss, everything from lime-green bird's nest ferns (*Asplenium australasicum*) to whisper-soft native maidenhair (*Adiantum aethiopicum*). Lush green paddocks (not so much mown lawns) are also very relaxing.

Ponds, waterlilies and fish are superbly relaxing.

5. **Birds:** Whack in some grevilleas and banksias and kangaroo paws. Then sit back and watch the spinebills, honeyeaters, wattlebirds and all their mates line up to feed. Our robins regularly spend hours in our garage hunting spiders and insects. They assemble when I dig the ground and wait for worms or insects to be thrown their way. They confidently expect excavations to cease as they dive in to snap up wrigglies. And excavations do cease as I drink in the serenity.

The greens of soft, velvety moss and ferns are just so calming.

6. **The Gate:** Bridie Prettijohn once said to me, 'Don't forget to lean on the gate.' She has gone now, but she was right. Stop to smell the roses. Lean on gates, plant vast numbers of perfumed plants. And relax.

Plant some grevilleas, banksias and kangaroo paws and soon you'll have honeyeaters like this and more of his feathered friends in your backyard.

CHAPTER 6
Sex in the suburbs

*G*ardens are steamy places full of procreation, intrigue, cheating, emotions, memories and sex. Yes, sex. Dangerous liaisons.

In a great garden sex is always just around the corner. Take Liss and Scott. They both work long hours, both really successful young people—the sort of people any family or country for that matter would be proud of. They have three kids and he dragged along three other sprogs from his last relationship.

Their lives are insanely busy, deeply satisfying, but a whorl of nappies and kids' schooling through to puberty wars. They have lost the romantic evenings (Kai has a rash and diarrhoea), impromptu sex (he used to sneak around to visit her in her bedroom at her parents' place late at night) and sex has taken a back seat in their lives. Very different from the back seat adventures they had when they were dating.

And Esme and Bill, they've been married for 45 years. There's no romance in their lives any more. Lots of kindness, heaps of cooperation, but no danger. No spark. And no spank.

'Consider the lilies of the field. Behold the birds of the air, for they neither sow, nor do they reap nor gather into barns; and your heavenly Father feedeth them. Are you not of much more value than they?' (Life of Brian and Matthew 6:26 and 28.) Well, those wretched little birds of the air sneak off into the bushes when no-one is looking. The gloriously monogamous blue wren lives an exquisitely moral family life with dad, mum and the kids that join in raising their younger brothers and sisters. But 40 per cent of the eggs don't come from dad. Mum sneaks off for dangerous liaisons. The same happens with the devotedly monogamous zebra finch. Infidelity is the norm in monogamous animals and, sadly, DNA research into long-married human couples has shown that 20–40 per cent of the kids don't come from dad either.

The Alhambra.

The Alhambra is my favourite garden in the world. This part of it is called The Generalife: it has been copied all over the world.

Why? Clearly bad gardens are to blame. Does your garden have sex in it? St Matthew again has the answer: 'Be not solicitous therefore, saying What shall we eat; or What shall we drink; or Wherewith shall we be clothed? For after all these things do the heathens seek. For your heavenly Father knoweth that you have need of all these things.' (Matthew 6:31-2.)

Your Heavenly Father knows that you need to eat, drink and be naked. So it's okay. Especially for Liss, Scott, Esme and Bill. But how? Well, the Arab Sheikh Nefgaoui has the answer: 'The Perfumed Garden'. I learned horticulture from this learned treatise. Perfumed gardens are the most important part of world horticulture. My world's No. 1 garden is the Red Fort, known by its Spanish/Arabian name of the Alhambra. It is in Granada in Spain and was a pleasure dome for the Sultan Muhammad V (1353–1391).

Here, perfumed plants and pools of water dominate. Perfume captivates you; entrances and excites you. It reaches into the deep recesses of the brain and enlivens them.

My No. 1 perfumed plant? It's all over Spain: think Valencia or Seville. Streets and streets of oranges. The citrus tree is the world's sexiest plant. Lusty, glossy leaves, a sensuous perfume from the virginal white flowers, then beautifully scented fruit that are a triumph to eat. No wonder to this very day we have oranges called Valencia, Seville… and Navel.

The Alhambra is full of superb roses, citrus everywhere and every perfumed plant known to man (in Europe at that time). So let's look at our marital aids: perfumed plants.

Left: Valencia oranges.

Perfumed plants

Citrus: Oranges, lemons, limes, mandarins, grapefruit, cumquats and finger limes.

- Mandarins are the best fruit for kids. They are very sweet and easy to peel. All gardeners should be required to have a mandarin and a lemon tree. BY LAW!
- Red grapefruit are better than the old ones (Wheeny and Marsh) so select Rio Red, Star Ruby, Flame, etc. These are sweeter, superior varieties.

A: Mandarins are the best fruit for kids.

B: Mandarins are super sweet and really easy for kids to peel.

- Finger limes (Aussie plants) are really, really good. They're thorny mongrels with ugly, small blackish fruit about the size of your little finger. Inside they are weird. Cut the fruit in half, and spoon or squeeze out stuff like pink caviar. Little pearls of explosive lime flavour. Pick out the odd seed and use the pearls on oysters, on hors d'oeuvres, in drinks, in jams…

You name it. Very stylish and very tasty. Recipes over the page:

A: The finger lime plants are thorny mongrels but the fruit is incredible.

B: Inside a finger lime, its guts are like caviar. Tiny pearls of explosive lime flavour.

C: Simply squeeze out the finger lime pulp, pick out the odd seed and it's ready to use.

Finger lime fruit are, predictably enough, about the size of your fingers.

A savoury
sensation.

Canapes

Savoury

Mix:
250g softened or room temperature cream cheese
1 cup loosely packed chopped coriander
A pinch of both salt and pepper
Garnish with finger lime pulp

Serve on crackers

Garnish with finger lime pulp.

Sweet

Mix:
250g mascarpone cheese
½ cup icing sugar
Garnish with strawberries and finger lime pulp.

Finger lime pulp can also be added to punch, added chilled to oysters and used with hors' d'oeuvres.

Spoon on some finger lime pulp to oysters naturale.

A winning combination.

The finger lime brings a
zesty tang to these sweet treats.

Finger limes can be purchased from Daleys Fruit Trees–www.daleysfruit.com.au or Engall's Nursery in Sydney–997 Old Northern Road, Dural (02) 9651 2735

Roses: Thorny mongrels, but there are thornless varieties around (check our Wallara Roses–www.wallararoses.com.au). Make sure you ask for highly perfumed thornless ones. If you can tolerate the thorns, try:

- 'Amber'
- 'Brindabella Bouquet'
- 'Duchesse de Brabant'
- 'Ebb Tide'
- 'Ferdinand Pichard'
- 'Gruss an Aachen'
- 'Madame Alfred Carriere'
- 'Mayor of Casterbridge'
- 'The Mayflower'
- 'Scentuous'

Our top two perfumed roses are:

- 'Oklahoma'
- 'Charles de Gaulle'

Our top perfumed rose 'Oklahoma'.

Murraya: *Murraya paniculata* must be Australia's most popular shrub. It's a relative of citrus trees and it has even better white perfumed flowers. In cooler zones substitute *Choisya ternata*, as it is much the same.

Heliotrope: *Heliotropium arborescens*. Awesome violet or mauve flowers with a wondrous vanilla-like perfume. This shrub only grows around 1m tall.

Daphne: *Daphne odora*. A breathtakingly powerful perfume, reminiscent of citrus. A cantankerous mongrel to grow in all but the mountain or cool zones. Better in a pot in temperate zones like Sydney, but use Yates Anti-Rot to prolong its life.

Osmanthus: *Osmanthus fragrans*. Size doesn't always count. The flowers of this plant are very tiny, almost invisible but they waft apricot perfume all around. Sex on a stick.

Geraniums: Most geraniums stink, but the perfumed ones are out of this world. Technically they are pelargoniums and their leaves smell wonderful. The peppermint-leafed geranium smells far better than genuine peppermint. But there are rose-scented geraniums (used to produce the world's rose oil), lemon-scented geraniums, even nutmeg! Cheap, easy to grow and very romantic. As you brush past them or tread on a leaf (they are low plants) you will be transported–no need to 'Beam me up, Scottie'.

Lemon-scented myrtle: *Backhousia citriodora* is a lillypilly relative that has a better lemon perfume than lemons. It is excellent for cooking or deodorising.

Lavender: Maybe the most romantic perfume of all. The leaves and flowers have this glorious perfume and the silver-coloured leaves are very beautiful. Great for hedges or in pots.

Winter honeysuckle: Smells pretty much the same as daphne, but it is much, much easier to grow. It is a shrub, not a climber and it has a rather open growth habit. In winter the perfume carries over huge distances. *Lonicera fragrantissima* is its name. It is hard to get, but it is a stunner.

Violets: Cunning bastards these. Most of them don't pong. But the ones that do are magnificent. The native one has very little perfume, although some wild forms in the bush are nicely perfumed. The plain deep purple forms of *Viola odorata* are probably best and the varieties 'Purple Robe' or 'Royal Robe' are usually strongly perfumed. Some parma violets are perfumed too. Buy *only* when they are in flower, and select with your nose.

Silky myrtle: Impossible to purchase this Aussie native in nurseries, but it has a lovely perfume from its tiny, white flowers. *Decaspermum fruticosum* is its botanic name. It looks like and is related to lillypillies and it grows around 6m tall.

Port wine magnolia: (*Michelia figo*) Smells of Juicy Fruit chewing gum. The white flowering variety of this, called 'Coco' is much better. There are lots of michelias (relos of magnolias) and all are beautifully perfumed. *M. doltsopa* 'Silver Cloud' is very good, but then all michelias are.

Jonquils: These are probably the hardiest, strongly-perfumed plants in the world. 'Erlicheer' is the best. They are bulbs that flower in winter.

Brown boronia: *Boronia heterophylla*–a native shrub with brown cup-shaped flowers with a bright yellow inner colour. Red, yellow and other flower colours exist. Stunning citrus-like perfume. Mongrel of a plant to grow except in South Australia or Western Australia.

Star jasmine: *Trachelospermum jasminoides.* Not a true jasmine and therefore not a weed. Vanilla perfume, glossy leaves and not too vigorous. Great climber for any use.

Gardenia: Oozes sex this plant. Lovely white flowers, delicious sweet perfume for most of the year. *Gardenia augusta* 'Florida' is the best one.

Jasmine: Lots of these strongly perfumed plants, but most are invasive weeds in the garden. *Jasminum sambac* 'Grand Duke of Tuscany' is a wonderful perfumed shrub for warmer areas. Highly recommended.

Lilac: For cooler and mountain zones only. Large flower heads with a delicious perfume in white pink or purple. Small trees to about 4m tall.

Luculia: From the Himalayas, a rich vanilla-like perfume. Grows around 4m (13ft) tall, loves a bit of lime, loves to drop dead too. Pink or white hydrangea-like flower heads.

Rhododendrons: Tropical (Vireya) types. Usually the white flowering varieties smell like gardenias.

Stephanotis: *Stephanotis floribunda*. A sub-tropical climber with white, highly-scented flowers. Great in a pot.

Viburnums: These are shrubs around 2–5m (6.5–16ft) tall. Most are nicely perfumed. Good privacy plants.

Philadelphus: Shrubs growing to 3m (10ft) or so with round, white perfumed flowers. Graceful and useful plants. Several species but *Philadelphus x virginalis* 'Virginal' is probably the best.

Sex and cheating
(Don't read this if cheating offends you)

On special days (visitors due or you are down in the dumps) why not cheat on your spouse. It's so easy. Get some lavender oil, orange oil, rose oil, peppermint oil, lemon-scented myrtle oil, mandarin oil, jasmine oil, lime oil, ginger oil, bergamot oil or whatever. Nearly fill your atomiser bottle with water, add a small amount of your aromatic oil then a few drops of 'essential oil dispersant' or Solubalizer and shake well. The oil will form an emulsion in the water and is ready to use.

Now, spray around paths, pots, on walls, etc. with the atomiser bottle and the whole area will come alive. Improve your lavender with lavender oil. Pump up the roses with rose oil, help out your citrus, your mints and all of the rest. You can spray directly on the plants. It won't hurt them.

A: Select some essential oils and get a bottle of Solubalizer or essential oil dispersant.

B: Nearly fill up an atomiser bottle with water and add a few drops of your favourite essential oil.

C: Then add a few drops of Solubalizer.

D: Put the nozzle on and shake well.

E + F: Spray around your pots, using a lavender mix for your lavenders.

G: You can also spray along paths, for a perfumed stroll.

H: Or even spray your fence.

Now, isn't that better than using one of those foul toilet sprays in the loo? You will now have an instant highly perfumed garden. These perfumes often last for a week or more and NO-ONE will ever know how you cheated…UNLESS they read this book. The odds of that happening are pretty low anyway.

Lastly, just wait for things to happen.

CHAPTER 7
Pentecostal gardening

'Yea brother, I beseech unto you that you place your faith in organics. The devil has created genetically modified crops, plant patenting, artificial fertilisers, hybrid vegetables, toxic sprays and evil commercial exploitation of the masses.'

'But the lord hath invented biodynamics, organic gardening, worm farms, recycling, sunshine and wind. Evil shall engulf those who refuse to follow the Lord's path. Hell is a paddock full of GM corn.'

So pontificated Erasmus Bligh, the founder of Composter's Seeds recently. He leads a group of Pentecostal Gardeners. He rails against the evils of the other seed companies and multinationals in general… and he has a product to sell you that will redress all of the evils of the world. Pay him money, adopt his religion, change your life and you will be very rich indeed (and so will he). He can send you out salvation in a brown paper bag for $11.75 a plant.

And Erasmus does give value for money. Buy his stuff, follow his Pentecostal Gardening tenets and you will feel so much better about the planet and the starving hordes in Africa. They will still be starving, but you will feel better. The planet will still be warming, but you will feel better. The pandas will still be dying but you will feel better.

For all that, not everything Erasmus teaches is wrong (money aside for the moment). Sure, biodynamics is a wacky religion that has no basis in truth in the real world. Sure, GM crops are set to save millions of lives in the poor countries of the world. Sure, hybrid vegies are just as good as any others and plant patenting has its good side as well as some bad aspects. But some of Erasmus's ideas…well, no, they aren't his ideas, he borrowed them from others. But the ideas, some of them, are worth pursuing, so here follows a look at the other world of organic gardening and food production. Minus the religious stuff. Just plain good health and good sense.

Growing vegies is the most popular gardening activity in Australia today. With our bodies being bombarded by preservatives, food colouring, MSG, pesticides, fungicides, antibiotics, pollution, gases from paint and plastics and thousands of other contaminants, we are all anxious to cut back on the nasties as much as we can. Hence the quite sensible trend towards growing vegies at home.

This chapter is dedicated to those who want to grow organic vegies at home, free from artificial fertilisers, pesticides and fungicides. Particularly to those who want to give their kids a good start in life.

When I first started growing vegies, it was very hit and miss. I mucked up a lot of things, particularly fertilising. My first crops of radishes and silverbeet that I grew as a kid were okay the first season, but after that it all started to peter out. Most garden plants survive pretty well on neglect—not so vegies. Vegies need constant care with exactly the right feeding and attention. A bit like a newborn baby. Most garden plants in most areas will thrive without any fertiliser and precious little water—not so vegies.

So, welcome to your new world. When I failed to fertilise my leaf vegies like silverbeet they all bolted to seed. That is, I produced very few leaves to eat. When I failed to deal with caterpillars, I produced very few leaves to eat. When I planted my leaf vegies in part shade, they got fungal disease and, you get it, I went hungry.

Vegies need good soil preparation, full sun, regular and constant fertilising and some form of pest control. By regular I mean an inspection daily or every second day and some serious maintenance once a week: every week.

At the end of this chapter, we have our guide to fertilising fruit and vegies. For the moment all you need to know is that the label on most fertilisers can be very misleading. Organic fertiliser may not mean that the fertiliser is free of artificial, non-organic components. Don't forget that in 1993 we tested brands of blood and bone on *Burke's Backyard* and found that most were very impure and one had no blood and no bone in it at all. Our program forced changes in various laws governing fertilisers but you still need to be very careful.

Mind you, organic labels on fresh fruit and vegies at supermarkets are often very dubious. On several occasions we prepared stories on organic produce certification schemes to go to air on *Burke's Backyard*. None went to air because we found them all to be unsatisfactory. We didn't want to damn something we agreed with in principle, but we couldn't support dodgy practices. Hopefully things are improving.

I will try to deal with pest and disease control. The best pest and disease control comes from growing the most suitable vegies for your area in a well-prepared soil with excellent nutrition plus your vigilance. Some vegies simply won't do well where you live: so don't grow them. Swapping your excess vegies with vegies from neighbours is really smart. You grow beans and Chinese greens and your neighbour does the tomatoes and capsicums.

The problem with organic pest control is that it often doesn't work very well. You may need to spray with milk or garlic every 2–3 days, but simply don't have the time. If retailers sold pesticides like this, their customers would put them out of business. But if some dotty old dear up the road recommends them, you tend to forgive and forget. A bit like the very popular old lady's cleaning tips that don't work all that well: no-one is going to crucify her.

So I will try to steer a safe but sensible course.

Over 25 years ago when I tried to urge people to use less and safer pesticides, people got very angry with me: 'Don't you know what spray to use?' they'd yell. When I said that they didn't need chemicals, they'd hang up on radio. Over the intervening years I approached the Federal Government to set up a national body to control agricultural and veterinary chemicals to make things safer for all Australians and to improve the lot of animals as well. Primary Industries Minister at the time, Simon Crean, and I collaborated to set up what became known as the Australian Pesticides and Veterinary Medicines Authority and I served on the board for about five years. This has done many things, but one of the best was to remove the DDT family of chemicals due to their persistence in the environment. Simon Crean deserves an Order of Australia for his brilliant and tenacious work on this. Things are so much better now.

You need to develop a special neighbourhood to grow vegies well. In an ideal neighbourhood, all the predatory insects control most of the pests. If your neighbour uses nasty pesticides, it will be hard for you to encourage your ladybirds, birds, wasps and spiders who do 90 per cent of the pest work for you.

And this, dear reader, is where you discover what a devious mongrel I am. My dirty tricks consist of convincing neighbours to feed the native birds by planting native plants like grevilleas, banksias and kangaroo paws. Then to subtly point out that chemical sprays kill native birds (which is true). Soon people stop spraying and, at first, the vegies get slaughtered. Six months or so later, all the good insects and birds breed up and start controlling the pests better than ever. You will still get the odd outbreak of aphids or caterpillars, but the problems are not as bad as before.

So, in Chapter 15 I will list some of the least toxic sprays to beat the pests in emergencies. I hope I am not the dotty old dear that peddles silliness. I hope my stuff will work for you. I should point out that the dotty old dear is far more precious to me than the vigorous old gent of the past who used every toxic chemical known to man. Both of them meant well.

And you? Keen to do your bit for Australia? Okay.

Enough of the greenhouse gas belching plane trips to Bali. Time to consider more enriching pursuits. Forget the Pilates, power walking and social cappuccinos. Time to grow food. Pure, uncontaminated by toxic sprays, utterly organic produce. Flexibility and fitness will also come to the family with the stretching, bending, carrying, barrowing and kneeling to pick the vegies you've grown. It's all an investment in a long healthy future for young Sunday, Willow and Thugg.

Growing herbs and vegies at home is a wonderful experience for the whole family. It's a very precise work though. There are many ways of doing it, but we will look at three. Vegies and herbs mixed into the garden, those grown in a modern vegie garden and those grown in pots or containers.

Mixed into the garden

There's no reason you can't sneak attractive vegies into your general garden area. Remember that they need full sun all day. Some of the prettiest and best herbs to grow in the general garden are:

- Basil
- Chives
- Shallots
- Parsley
- Oregano
- Thyme
- Rosemary

Coriander is short lived and best grown between April and September in pots (in warmer weather it bolts to seed. If you wish, these seeds can be collected and ground up in a mortar and pestle for use in Asian dishes). Mints tend to go feral and they are far too rapacious to plant in the ground. Confine these delicious mongrels to pots.

There are many many vegies that look good in the garden: ornamental or plain silverbeet (aka chard), Asian greens (wombok or Chinese cabbage is superb), cos lettuce, climbing beans (on a fence), chillies, pumpkins (in a ramshackle garden), carrots, even blousy eggplants.

There's no reason you can't sneak attractive herbs and vegies in amongst your normal plants as has been done in this garden.

A few traps though. Vegies and herbs should not be grown near most native plants. Grevilleas, banksias and hakeas really hate strong fertilisers. If you must grow vegies near them—stick to a small amount of Dynamic Lifter (the original formula, not the Fruit & Citrus formula) and liquid doses of Nitrosol.

In a modern vegie garden

The potager garden is the best of all vegie gardens. This is a gridded series of long, narrow beds—serviced all around by sturdy paths. We laid second-hand bricks for our potager garden and sparged the inside edges of the bricks with 3:1 sand/cement mortar to stop the bricks collapsing. The bricks were laid on coarse sand and the sand left over was mixed with the soil in the plots.

Even when empty, the potager garden looks good. As you harvest your vegies they are all easy to reach and your shoes stay clean. Civilised vegies!

In a modern potager vegie garden, you can grow all vegies and all herbs and none can escape and become weeds. Remember that Asian greens are far better than the European ones. Wombok, the upright Chinese cabbage, grows in about half the time taken by European cabbages. You can also grow two to four times as many Womboks per square metre. They look far more attractive and make a crunchier coleslaw and don't stink the house out when you cook them. They also

The potager garden is the best of all vegie gardens.

demand less fertilisers and need less pest control and spraying, as do all the Asian greens. There is Asian broccoli and lots of other Asian greens worth a try.

There are miniature European cabbages and cauliflower which are good, but I think the Asian varieties are better. True spinach and mini spinach are excellent also.

Consider sugar snap peas ahead of snow peas. Sugar snap peas are sweeter, crunchier and less stringy. Super-sweet corn is the best–particularly for the kids. Potatoes are loads of fun, very easy and special home varieties are much tastier. Consult some of the mail-order mobs for home varieties.

Potatoes are best treated as an annual crop. Plant the so-called seed potatoes, which are just the tubers that we eat, in Spring. While you can harvest earlier if you wish, normally the potatoes are dug up, ie harvested, around January or February when they tend to die down naturally. New potatoes are harvested earlier on, about 3–4 weeks after the plants have flowered, just when some of the lower leaves are yellowing.

A: Really fluff up your soil and dig a trench about 30cm deep.

B: After you have dried your potato pieces in a shady spot for a week or two, they are ready to plant.

Cut your seed potatoes into large pieces with at least one eye per piece.

A: Plant the potato pieces about 30-40cm apart.

B: Shovel soil on top and scatter fertiliser such as Dynamic Lifter or citrus or rose food.

C: In the months ahead, the potato plants will become quite large. They have reached full maturity when the plant starts to yellow off. See Chapter 8 for a useful guide to harvesting all your vegies.

Potatoes are grown in soil that has been really fluffed-up, that is, dug to around 30cm (12in) deep. I like to dig in as much compost or horse stable manure as I can get, some weeks in advance of planting. The seed potatoes should be cut into large pieces, with at least one eye per piece. Perhaps two to four pieces from each tuber. Much as you do with frangipani cuttings, spread the pieces out to dry in a shady spot for a week or two before planting.

Plant the pieces of tuber about 30-40cm (12-16in) apart and 10cm (4in) deep. Scatter any general fertiliser over the ground (citrus or rose food or Dynamic Lifter) and lightly water it in. Do not soak the soil at planting time.

Potato sprouts should emerge in three to four weeks. As they grow, rake soil up to the base of the plant to provide stability for the bush, and room for more tubers to grow. This creates a hill around the base of each plant. This practice would be disastrous with any other garden plant but potatoes and tomatoes love it.

Pumpkins, zucchinis and cucumbers love to ramble and need lots of space. In a large rambling garden, pumpkins look wonderful and you can get some spectacular varieties such as 'Jarrahdale' (large size) or 'Butternut' (smaller 1–2kg) fruit. There are bush pumpkins which are compact and smaller-growing such as 'Golden Nugget', which spread about 1m (3ft) or so and which are excellent in tubs. It produces up to 10 small, round pumpkins. For best keeping, ie. long-lasting pumpkins, do not harvest until the vine has died off (see the When to Pick Fruit Guide in Chapter 8).

Tomatoes are great to grow at home. They need constant work, but the flavours are always fantastic. Be very clear on this, the smaller cherry-fruited varieties are much easier and better to grow.

Of all the vegies you grow at home, tomatoes are both the most rewarding and the most popular. The homegrown varieties are superbly tasty—far exceeding the taste and texture of fruit from the supermarket. Nothing equals the experience of swanning out into the backyard, grabbing a luscious red tomato off the bush, then slicing it up and eating it—with a leaf of basil from your herb garden and perhaps a slice of bocconcini on top.

Tomatoes need constant work and good growing conditions, but in return they produce more fruit for their size than any other plant.

Yet 20 years ago, few people grew them at home and very few varieties were readily available. In 1987 on *Burke's Backyard* I grabbed a ripe Floradade tomato (the most common one in supermarkets at the time) and kept hitting it against a brick wall with a tennis racquet while I talked about the pathetic taste of this variety. After a couple of minutes of hitting I caught it and held it up to the camera. Not a mark on it! It lasted forever but did not taste like a tomato.

This led to a rapid and complete change in tomato growing. People started demanding tastier tomatoes and growers responded. Seed companies also started to make better varieties available to their customers.

Today there are hundreds of varieties available and home gardeners get into arguments over the best tasting tomato varieties all of the time. In truth, different varieties do better in different areas. They vary in insect resistance, disease resistance, climatic preferences and soil likes and dislikes. So a variety that is superb in Hamilton, Victoria may not taste so good in Buderim Queensland. In fact, you can cross the road and encounter a different microclimate and different soils and hence different flavour.

But what the hell, they are cheap to buy and fun to grow, so try out several varieties this year at your place.

While tomatoes are usually sold as vegies, they are in fact fruit, as are beans, peas, cucumbers, eggplants, melons, pumpkins, corn, zucchinis, chillies and capsicums.

Cherry tomatoes are by far the easiest to grow: they are much hardier and more disease resistant. In general, cherry tomato varieties are more cold tolerant and will often grow into or through winter, unlike their larger-fruited cousins which cark it quickly in cold weather. The smaller-fruiting varieties have a tougher skin and are a bit more fruit fly resistant too.

There are many varieties of heirloom tomatoes. In general, they are old varieties that are not suitable for production for supermarkets: either they don't travel well or they crop over too long a period leading

Yellow pear tomato.

Cherry tomatoes.

to commercial harvesting difficulties. Nonetheless the heirloom varieties are really good for growing at home. Often they taste far better than commercial varieties, and cropping over a long period is very desirable in the home garden.

For taste 'Rumsey's Red' or 'Rumsey's Cross' are hard to beat. Hard to buy too, as they are very uncommon—try www.roystonpetrieseeds. com.au. 'Burnley Sweetcrop' is an excellent heirloom variety, great flavour and huge trusses of fruit available from www.seedsavers.net.

Other good varieties are: 'Australian Red' (E); 'Black Krim' (E, O, R, D); 'Amish Paste' (E, D); 'Kotlas' (E); 'Roma San Marzano' (G, R); 'Beefsteak' (O); 'Burke's Backyard Italian Tomato' (N,Y); 'Oxheart' (N, G, R, D); 'KY1' (R); 'ES58' (R); 'Mortgage Lifter' (D, R); 'Tropic' (R). 'Amish Paste' (D, E) and 'Roma San Marzano' are egg-shaped Roma types that are excellent for cooking into sauces, etc.

A: Amish Paste.

B: Black Krim.

C: Kotlas. Photos courtesy
Eden Seeds.

Cherry tomatoes

Most of these are superb plants–so easy to grow and so good in containers. Some recommended varieties are: 'Sweetie' (N, R); 'Cherry Fox' (E); 'Tiny Tim' (N, R, Y) 'Sweet 100' (R); and 'Tommy Toe' (N, S, R, D).

Key

N = Local nurseries
S = www.seedsavers.net
G = www.greenharvest.com.au
R = www.roystonpetrieseeds.com.au
D = www.diggers.com.au
O = www.roguelands.com
Y = www.yates.com.au
E = www.edenseeds.com.au

(Note: The seed suppliers above carry a wide
range of seeds in addition to tomato seeds)

Growing tomatoes

A: In temperate regions (Sydney, Perth) you can sow tomato seeds prior to spring in a protected area such as inside the house on a windowsill. First, choose a tomato seed.

B + C: Sow your seeds in a seedling tray or punnet with a seed raising mix. Make small holes with your fingers or a pencil or skewer and plant the seeds 3-4cm apart.

D + E: Cover the seeds and water.

F: Place the tray or punnet on a windowsill inside or in a protected spot outside.

G: Once your tomato seedlings are up, and the winter frosts are gone, they can be planted in the garden.

A: Plant tomatoes about 60cm apart in the garden.

B: Tomatoes are normally tied loosely to a 1.8m garden stake.

Tomatoes are basically scrambling semi-climbers. That is, they need some sort of support (don't we all?). These normal types are often called 'indeterminate types' to confuse you. The indeterminate types keep on climbing and growing and fruiting over a long period and are the best home varieties. They need staking and tying up as they grow.

Determinate varieties tend to grow into a bush, don't need much staking and crop over a shorter period—so they are ideal for commercial production.

Tomatoes die in cold weather and frosts are bad for them, so don't plant until the danger of frosts is gone. They need a three-month growing season, so, in frost-free northern areas, you can plant them all year round. In temperate regions (Sydney, Perth) sow seeds in a protected area (on a windowsill inside or in a warm, protected spot outside) in August/September and a later crop in November. This way you'll get fruit from mid-December to mid-April. In cold areas sow seed September to November.

Sow your seeds in a seedling tray or a punnet and transplant them into the garden (if frosts are gone) or into 10cm (4in) pots for growing on (if it's still cold). Plant tomatoes about 60cm (24in) apart in the garden. Prepare the garden soil by digging over and digging in about two handfuls of Dynamic Lifter per square metre. Excessive nitrogen may cause problems later on, so be careful.

Don't fertilise again until the first truss of fruit has set. Then apply a tablespoon of general fertiliser every four or five weeks and water it in well every time. Tomatoes need twice-a-week thorough watering as the plant grows and the fruit develop.

Normally tomatoes are tied to a 1.8m (6ft) garden stake. Most people allow two main stems and both are loosely tied to the stake. To feed an average family, you'll need twelve or more plants. You could choose to plant them in rows or groups, hammering in a stake at each corner and running string or wire along the sides to keep the plants supported. Some people use concrete reinforcing mesh to cage or tie the plants against.

Vegies in pots or containers

You can easily grow herbs or vegies even if you don't have a garden at all.

1. Select any old container lying about: we found some old ceramic tile boxes made of timber, but terracotta pots, ceramic pots or anything else will do.

2. Drill some drainage holes in the bottom if there aren't any already.

3. Mix 50/50 potting mix and coarse sand (this is ideal for continued cropping over several years or it can be used after harvesting the plants as a superb soil conditioner or general potting mix). Chuck it into the container.

4. Bung in seeds or seedlings. We chose Asian greens (quick and easy and they get fewer pests and diseases), mixed herbs and strawberries in our three boxes.

5. For each group of six seedlings, sprinkle on the surface of the potting mix a handful of Dynamic Lifter for Fruit & Citrus and also one handful of cow manure and water in thoroughly.

6. Water every second day and also once a week with a mixture of Nitrosol and Seasol at standard rates together in the same watering can.

7. Start to harvest in about three weeks.

Important: Vegies must be grown in full sun

A: Select an old container (we found three old timber tile boxes) and drill drainage holes if none already exist. Fill it up with a 50/50 mix of potting mix and coarse sand. This mix is ideal for continued cropping over several years or can be used after harvesting as a superb soil conditioner or general potting mix.

B: For our three boxes we chose strawberries, mixed herbs and Asian greens (which are quick and easy and they get fewer pests and diseases).

D: For each group of six seedlings sprinkle on a handful of Dynamic Lifter for Fruit and Citrus and a handful of cow manure.

E: Water in thoroughly.

F: Water every second day and also once a week with a mixture of Nitrosol and Seasol at standard rates together in the same watering can.

Right: They look fantastic in these old boxes and will be ready to harvest in about three weeks.

Vegies not worth bothering with

Celery is cheap in the shops and complex to grow. Cabbages are also cheap to buy in the fruit shop, very slow growing (3–4 months from seed), and dead-set ugly, as are broccoli and cauliflower. Mini carrots are a bit of fun for the kids, but most root crops like parsnips, swedes, etc. are not worth the trouble. Garlic is problematic to grow, although onions are okay. Sweet potatoes tend to take over the garden, as do most mints.

Fertilising fruit and vegies

Beware of naughty labelling. Under the various state laws in Australia, many fertilisers are labelled as organic when they are only partly organic. That is, they contain synthetic ingredients as well as the natural, organic ones. Always check for the statement '100% Organic' of 'BFA Organic Registered Product' or 'Australian Certified Organic'.

The ridgy-didge pure, 100 per cent organic fertilisers are:

- The still available, original formula of Dynamic Lifer (pellets)
- Amgrow Organic Harvest (Liquid)
- Cow manure
- Horse manure
- Poultry manure
- Most other manures

Dynamic Lifter is both composted and pasteurised–it is perhaps the only organic bagged product that can't give you Legionnaire's Disease, coccidiosis, salmonella, etc. It may still contain very small amounts of artificial food or drugs fed to the chooks.

Amgrow Organic Harvest is fish and seaweed based. It also contains the most powerful natural plant growth hormone, Triacontanol.

All animal manures may contain traces of artificial foods or drugs fed to the animals such as antibiotics, worming agents and growth hormones.

For the record, blood and bone is an excellent mostly organic fertiliser, but it may contain some artificial additives. Nitrosol, which is a very good liquid fertiliser based on blood and bone, also contains artificial fertiliser additives.

So what does all this mean? The concept of 100% pure organic is fine, and you can reasonably choose this type. I have no problem with using Nitrosol (which also contains Triacontonal, the natural growth promoter) and also no problems with Dynamic Lifter fortified pellets. That is, Dynamic Lifter with a small addition of extra synthetic fertilisers to balance the formula. I use Dynamic Lifter for Fruit & Citrus on my fruit and vegies. It's all a matter of personal choice.

Seasol, the seaweed extract, is 100% pure organic liquid, but it is more a root growth promoter and a plant health tonic than a fertiliser.

Anyway, all of this may help you to understand why I have recommended Dynamic Lifter, Seasol and Nitrosol for all of these years. I recommend them without any payments or other association much as *Choice* magazine recommends products.

Pests and diseases of fruit and vegies

Pests

Pest	Best treatment	Organic treatment
Caterpillars	Yates Success or Dipel	Yates Success or Dipel
Sucking insects, aphids, scale, etc.	Confidor & Pest Oil	Eco-oil
Fruit fly mites and whitefly	Eco Naturalure Pest Oil	Eco Naturalure Eco-oil
Snails and slugs	Multiguard	Multiguard (safe with pets and wildlife)

Diseases

Disease	Best treatment	Organic treatment
Powdery Mildew	Eco-rose	Eco-rose or milk (diluted 1:10 with water)
Other fungal diseases (Peach leaf curl, rust,etc.)	Kocide	Lime sulphur
Root Rot	Yates Anti Rot	Yates Anti Rot

Planting Calendar

This handy gardener's guide tells seed sowers when to sow and plant every popular flower and vegetable, Australia-wide.

Vegetables	Best months to sow seed — Cold (J F M A M J J A S O N D)	Best months to sow seed — Temperature (J F M A M J J A S O N D)	Best months to sow seed — Tropical–subtropical (J F M A M J J A S O N D)	Seed approximate time to harvest from sowing (weeks)	Seedlings, etc. approximate time to harvest from transplanting (weeks)
Artichoke (suckers)				#	20–28
Asparagus (crowns)				#	16–24
Bean (climbing)				10–12	9–10
Bean (dwarf)				8–10	6–8
Beetroot				0–12	6–8
Broad bean				18–20	12–16
Broccoli				12–16	8–10
Brussels sprouts				16–20	12–14
Cabbage				8–16	4–10
Capsicum (pepper)				14–16	6–8
Carrot				16–20	14–16
Cauliflower				14–26	10–20
Celery				20–22	12–14
Chicory				16–20	*
Chilli				10–12	8
Burke's Backyard Thai Chilli				10–12	8
Chinese broccoli				9–11	7–9
Chinese cabbage				8–10	4–6
Choko (sprouted fruit)				20–22	18–20
Cucumber				8–12	5–9
Eggplant				14–16	4–6

Best months to sow seed

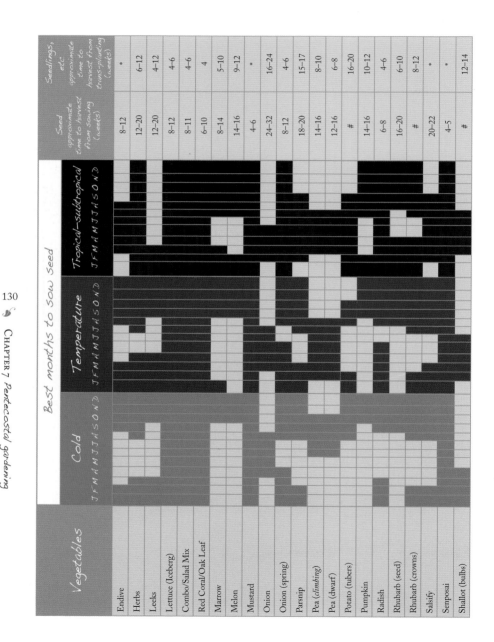

Vegetables	Cold JFMAMJJASOND	Temperature JFMAMJJASOND	Tropical–subtropical JFMAMJJASOND	Seed approximate time to harvest from sowing (weeks)	Seedlings, etc. approximate time to harvest from transplanting (weeks)
Endive				8–12	*
Herbs				12–20	6–12
Leeks				12–20	4–12
Lettuce (Iceberg)				8–12	4–6
Combo/Salad Mix				8–11	4–6
Red Coral/Oak Leaf				6–10	4
Marrow				8–14	5–10
Melon				14–16	9–12
Mustard				4–6	*
Onion				24–32	16–24
Onion (spring)				8–12	4–6
Parsnip				18–20	15–17
Pea (*climbing*)				14–16	8–10
Pea (dwarf)				12–16	6–8
Potato (tubers)				#	16–20
Pumpkin				14–16	10–12
Radish				6–8	4–6
Rhubarb (seed)				16–20	6–10
Rhubarb (crowns)				#	8–12
Salsify				20–22	*
Senposai				4–5	*
Shallot (bulbs)				#	12–14

Vegetables	Seed approximate time to harvest from sowing (weeks)	Seedlings, etc approximate time to harvest from transplanting (weeks)
Silver beet	8-12	4-6
Spinach	8-10	4-5
Squash	12-14	8-10
Sweet corn	12-16	9-12
Sweet potato (shoots)	#	18-20
Tomato	12-20	8-12
Turnip	10-12	6-10

not usually grown from seed by home gardeners * not widely available as a seedling (grow from seed)

Best months to sow seed

Flowers	Cold JFMAMJJASOND	Temperate JFMAMJJASOND	Tropical-subtropical JFMAMJJASOND	Seed approximate time to harvest from sowing (weeks)	Seedlings, etc approximate time to harvest from transplanting (weeks)
Ageratum				14	8
Alyssum				8	3
Amaranthus				14	7
Aster				14	8
Aurora daisy (*Arctotis*)				16	10
Balsam				8	3-4
Begonia, bedding				16	6
Calendula				10	5
Californian poppy (*Eschscholzia*)				8	3
Candytuft				12	6
Canterbury bells				14	6
Carnation				28	20
Celosia				12	6
Chrysanthemum				24	16

Plant		
Cineraria	20	12
Cockscomb	12	6
Coleus	10	4
Columbine (Aquilegia)	28	20
Cornflower (Centaurea)	14	8
Cosmos	12	6
Dahlia (seed)	16	10
Delphinium	20	12
Dianthus	20	14
English daisy (Bellis perennis)	12	6
Everlasting daisy (Acroclinium)	14	8
Geranium (seed)	16	6
Gerbera	30–50	18–35
Gloxinia	30	*
Gypsophila	10	4
Impatiens	12	4–6
Larkspur	20	12
Linaria	10	6
Livingstone daisy	20	13
Lobelia	14	6
Lupin	16–32	10–26
Marigold, African	12	6
Marigold, French	12	6
Marmalade daisy (Rudbeckia)	14	6
Nasturtium	10	8–10
Nemesia	14	6

Painted daisy	14	9
Pansy	16	8–9
Petunia	12	4–6
Phlox	10	4
Polyanthus	24	12
Poor man's orchid	14	8
Poppy, Iceland	24	18
Portulaca	6	0–2
Primula	24	14–16
Salpiglossis	12	6
Salvia	12	6–7
Snapdragon (*Antirrhinum*)	16	8–10
Spider flower (*Cleome*)	12	10
Statice	20	14
Stock	20	14
Strawflower (*Helichrysum*)	16	10–12
Sunflower (*Helianthus*)	12	10
Sweet pea	14	6
Sweet William	20	12
Torenia	16	10–12
Verbena	10	4
Viola	16	8–10
Virginian stock	14	8
Viscaria	12	*
Wallflower	24	18
Zinnia	12	8

CHAPTER 8

If you pick it, it will never get better

*T*hat's what my mum told me. 'For God's sake, leave it alone'.
But picking is one of life's great pleasures. But when should
you do it? Do you let the zucchinis get 1m long before picking? Why
aren't the citrus sweet? When do you pick pumpkins? Is a basketball-
sized radish any good?

A few general words first. The sweetest table grapes and oranges
come from Bourke in New South Wales. The oranges are really
sweet even when still growing in size and green in colour. Why?
Well, Bourke has a huge number of sunny days each year. More sun
than most areas of Australia. It also has warm nights that lock in the
sweetness. Sun produces sugar, warm nights lock it in the fruit. So, if
you live in Melbourne, which has lots of grey days, lots of cool days
too, the sugar production is way down. The longer you leave the fruit
on the tree, the sweeter it will get. But some grey years with lots of
grey days will produce lots of sour fruit.

Often your local vegie and fruit gardeners will know local tricks to
achieve a really good result. Tiny amounts of copper sulfate around
a citrus tree will often sweeten the fruit, for instance (about a level
dessert spoon to a mature orange tree, spread over the entire area
under the canopy). Maybe complete trace elements from the local
nursery will help.

Anyway, here follows a useful guide to harvesting vegies, herbs and
fruit. Email us if you have any tricks of your own: thelazygardener@
burkesbackyard.com.au

Fruits and vegetables can be divided into three convenient groups
for picking purposes:

- best when young, sweet and tender (before full-size)
- great either fully ripe, or when young
- only picked when fully ripe

Best when young, sweet and tender:

- Asian greens (eg, pak choy, choy sum, buck choy, gai choy, gai laan)
- Basil
- Button squash
- Cucumber
- Loose leaf lettuces
- Mesclun salad mixes
- Mibuna
- Mizuna
- Mustard
- Pak choy
- Radish
- Rocket
- Shallots
- Zucchini

Basil.

- **Asian greens** such as pak choy, choy sum, gai choy grow rapidly and the whole plant is harvested when 15–18cm (6-7in) tall.

- **Basil** is an annual herb that loves warm weather. While each plant could last a whole summer, the leaves lose sweetness as the plant gets older. So, the ideal is to grow basil rapidly and pick leaves when plants are only 15cm (6in) tall. So, it's much better to grow a succession of crops of basil through the summer, and harvest each of them when young.

- **Button squash, cucumber and zucchini** are very productive plants but each of these vegies will become tough and much less sweet if allowed to grow too big. A good size guide for each vegie is the size you see for sale in the shops. If these plants produce too much and you can't eat your crop, it's still preferable to pick them when young (give them to your neighbour or a friend). They'll keep on cropping and maybe next time round you'll be ready to enjoy them again.

- **Loose leaf lettuces** can either be grown to full size then harvested whole, or you can pick some leaves from the time the plant has about eight leaves (start picking leaves from the outside of the plant, not the inside). These are often called 'pick-and-come-again' lettuces.

- **Mibuna, mizuna and rocket** must be picked young, because they soon lose quality if allowed to grow too big. Rocket and mizuna both become hot and peppery when old, and mibuna becomes tough and tasteless. You can start removing a leaf or two from each plant when plants are only 8cm (3in) tall, or you can harvest the whole plant when 10–15cm (4-6in) tall.

- **Mustard** suffers from the same problem as rocket and mizuna, only worse. It can become very hot and peppery if allowed to grow as big as your hand. A rapid grower, it should always be harvested young (from about finger-length size), but a few small mustard leaves really do give a mixed-leaf salad a lift in flavour.

- **Radishes** also become hotter and tougher as they get bigger, so pull them up and eat them when still just bite-sized.

- **Shallots** can be harvested when they are the thickness of a pencil. You can start pulling them from this stage but they last quite well in the ground, although their taste does get stronger as they age.

Pick before or at full size

These vegies are wonderfully versatile because they give you several weeks to enjoy them. You don't have to worry about being swamped with a sudden glut and being forced to eat more than you'd like, or to just give them away. These include:

- Beetroot
- Broad beans
- Capsicums
- Carrots
- Lemon grass
- Onions
- Parsnips
- Potatoes
- Pumpkins
- Wombok (Chinese cabbage)

Carrots.

Beetroot can be harvested as 'baby beets' after about six weeks (and in fact the leaves of baby beets look great and taste fine in a mixed-leaf salad). Any time between then and maturity, which is about three months after sowing seed, you can pull out a beetroot and enjoy it. In fact, to get better value out of your vegie patch, it's a good idea to sow seed much closer than recommended on the packet, then progressively harvest baby beets—a tasty variation on 'thinning'—until the correct distance is achieved between plants. You still end up with a good crop of mature beetroots, but along the way you've had an extra crop of baby beets to enjoy.

Broad bean fans will insist that it's the baby broad beans that taste divine, when you harvest the small, immature pods and eat them whole. However, you can also leave the pods to develop to full maturity, which is about 18 weeks after planting seed. If you don't harvest when the pods are small, then wait until they're fully sized. Harvesting during the in-between period will just give you a crop of small beans but the pods will have toughened and won't be tender enough to eat.

Capsicums can be picked when young and green, partially ripe (yellowish) or fully ripe and red. There is a slight flavour difference between each stage of ripeness, and they do have the best, sweetest

CHAPTER 8 *If you pick it, it will never get better*

flavour when red, but green home-grown capsicums are still delicious either raw in salads, or cooked. To avoid damaging plants, always pick capsicums using secateurs to snip them from the bush. If you try to harvest by pulling them off, you might break a branch.

Carrots are a similar case to beetroots. You can start pulling out baby carrots only eight weeks after the green leaves first appear above the ground, but you can then leave them to grow for four to six months to full size (depending on the variety). And, of course, you can harvest them any time in between as well. See our tips on growing and thinning beetroots, because you can do the same thing with carrots, sowing them more thickly than stated on the packet, then thinning them out as baby carrots until you get to the desired plant spacings.

Lemon grass is grown for its juicy, lemon-flavoured lower stems. Old lemon grass still has a reasonable flavour, but it becomes very tough to slice or chop. So, to ensure that stems are young and tender, cut all the plants down to ground level every year in early October, just as the weather starts to warm. It's best to start harvesting stems from the outside of the clump whenever you need some, through spring, summer and autumn.

Lemon grass.

Onions give you the signal that they're ready for harvest when the leaves start to die off (that's usually about four months after the first green shoots appeared above the soil). However, you can pull out immature onions only two months after the first green shoots appear. These immature plants are called spring onions, and they are wonderfully sweet and tender, great in salads and in sauces for seafood.

Parsnips are slower growing than carrots, taking around 18 to 20 weeks to reach full size, but the same tips for growing carrots apply to parsnips. You can harvest them young, but parsnip lovers will always advise you to let the plants enjoy some really cold winter days before pulling any up because the cold helps to sweeten the parsnips. Never let parsnips stay in the ground too long or they become woody and sour. If in doubt, harvest early.

Potatoes have reached full maturity when the above-ground part of the plant starts to yellow and die off. These are the 'old potatoes' sold in shops, often with a dusting of soil on them. However, you can harvest young 'new potatoes' well before then, either by digging up a whole young plant or, if you're growing potatoes in straw, by 'bandicooting' your way under the plant and picking as many tubers off the plant as you need. The old, fully mature spuds have the strongest flavour, but home-grown new potatoes are still delicious.

Pumpkins can be picked when very small, when they are sweet and tender (many people refer to these young pumpkins as 'baby squash'). However, to harvest a full-size pumpkin, keep an eye on the vine. The stem attached to each pumpkin will begin to wither, becoming wrinkly and woody – that's the signal to harvest them. Use secateurs to remove the pumpkin from the vine, leaving some of the stem attached to the pumpkin (this helps to prevent rot). If you accidentally remove the stem from the pumpkin, eat that one first because it won't keep well. However, it's best to selectively harvest both young and old pumpkins. By leaving about three to five fruit to grow to maturity on each vine, you'll get a good crop of full-sized pumpkins. All the other fruit that appear should be harvested when at baby squash stage, giving you an extra 'crop' to enjoy along the way. If you leave every baby fruit that forms on the vine, then you'll end up with a lot of small pumpkins, but no large, fully-flavoured beauties.

Wombok (Chinese cabbage) is a much better backyard vegie than ordinary European cabbage: it takes up less room in the garden, it grows quicker, doesn't stink out the house when you cook it, makes the best cole slaw ever and is terrific in stir-fries, soups and lots of Asian dishes. And to top all that off, you can harvest womboks when young (about 18–20cm (7–8in) high), or wait until they reach maturity after about 8 to 10 weeks after sowing, when they're around 25–30cm (10–12in) high, or enjoy them any time in between. Harvest the whole plant each time.

Pick fully ripe:
- Apples
- Citrus (oranges, lemons, mandarins, limes)
- Corn
- Garlic
- Green beans
- Rhubarb
- Tomatoes

Corn.

For lots of backyard kitchen gardeners, the delicious flavour of home-grown fruit is what it's all about. It's the freshest and the best. Taste a home-grown vine-ripened tomato and you'll become an instant convert to the cause. But how do you tell when the fruit is ripe? Here's an easy test: try one. Just one. Taste it. Some fruits are very helpful because they fall from the tree when ripe. When you see a fruit fall, that's the time to start taste-testing, and probably harvesting. However, other fruits such as citrus can hang on the tree for ages, even when ripe. And fruits such as avocados never ripen on the tree. They only ripen after harvesting. You just pick avocados when they're a good size, then they'll ripen over the next week or so.

Apples ripen anywhere between three to six months after flowering, depending on the variety. It's important to let apples ripen on the tree because under-ripe apples will rarely develop a good flavour after picking. A ripe apple should come away from the tree easily, if you give it a twist. If you have to yank hard at the apple to pull it off the tree, it's not ripe. It isn't difficult to test ripeness. Just pick one fruit and taste it. If it's not ripe, then the other fruit on the tree won't be ripe, either. Taste is your best guide for harvesting and fruit colour is another good clue. As fruits ripen, they change colour. Fruit size isn't a great indicator, however. If a tree isn't carrying a lot of fruit, each fruit might be large. If a tree is carrying a large amount of fruit, each fruit might be relatively small. Next year, if a lot of fruit develop, remove about one-third of the pea-sized baby fruit and your next crop will be of much better-sized fruit.

Citrus fruits are great for backyard gardeners because there's a long period when you can pick as many as you need that day. However, it isn't all plain sailing with citrus, so you need to learn each plant's habits. For example, oranges and mandarins can look great, be a perfect size and colour, and still be sour. The solution is simple: leave the fruit on the tree for a few weeks more, cut back on the amount of water you're giving it (but not to the point of letting it wilt). The extra time and the drier soil should concentrate the sugars in the fruit and they should be ready for harvesting. Always do a taste test. With mandarins, don't leave them on the tree too long or they could become puffy and dry. Limes and lemons are easier to harvest. Just pick limes when they're green and pick lemons when they're yellow. Be careful not to damage the plants when picking fruit. If they don't come off easily with a gentle tug, get out a pair of secateurs and cut them from the tree.

Corn lovers say that you should have a pot of water boiling in the kitchen when you pick corn, so that you can rush each cob straight into the pot. They might be exaggerating, but they're right that corn tastes best when fresh. And corn isn't quite as forgiving as the other crops on our 'harvest when ripe' list. If you leave ripe corn on the plant too long it loses sweetness rapidly and become starchy. But there is a simple test you can do for picking corn. The silks on top of the cob will go dry and brown when the cobs ripen. And if you pull the leaves away from the cob to reveal some corn kernels on the cob, just push a thumbnail into a kernel or two. If you see milky fluid seep out, then the corn is ripe and that's what you're having for dinner that night! If the fluid which seeps out from your thumbnail test is clear, then the cob isn't quite ripe. Come back tomorrow and do the thumbnail test again.

Garlic will tell you that it's ready to harvest when its leafy tops start to collapse and die off. That should happen about five to six months after planting. Harvesting is easy: just dig up the bulbs, and hang them up to dry in a dry, airy spot (under a verandah is ideal).

Green beans can be picked at any stage but they're at their best when 15–20cm (6–8in) long. Old and stringy beans aren't great eating, so if these abundant cropping plants are producing too much, give the excess to your neighbours rather than letting them stay on the plant.

Rhubarb stems are picked in summer and autumn by pulling sharply downwards and outwards, when the stems are fully formed (and usually a rich red colour, although green rhubarb is sold in some nurseries and is fine to eat as well, even though it doesn't look right). During winter, rhubarb plants will die back fully in cold climates, but in milder zones they'll only partially die back in winter. In warmer zones they won't die back at all and stems can be harvested almost year round. However, do remember that rhubarb plants need some stems and leaves to keep on living, so aim to have a couple of rhubarb plants

Watermelons.

growing and only harvest two or three stems from each plant at any one time. It's also best to let young rhubarb plants grow for two full years before you first harvest any stems.

Tomatoes should come away from the vine with a gentle tug when they are full ripe and well coloured. If you have to tug on the fruit it's not fully ripe. You can harvest partially ripened fruit if you're worried about fruit fly or birds causing damage, and then it's best to ripen the fruit indoors in a spot which receives no direct sunlight.

Watermelons give off a couple of good, tell-tale signs of ripeness. The colour of the underside of the melon changes from green to yellow when it's ripe, and if you tap on the fruit with a knuckle of your hand, it should give a hollow sound.

Ripe and ready, some nifty tricks

Beating fruit fly–pick crops early

Fruit flies prefer to lay their eggs in ripe fruit, so with some crops you can beat the fruit fly by picking crops early. Fruits such as tomatoes, mangoes and pears can be picked when fully formed but still green. Take them inside and they'll ripen nicely over the next week or so.

Early and late apples

The so-called 'late-season' apples have the longest storage life, and the 'early-season' apples have the shortest storage life – you should eat these soon after picking. If you want to store your late-season apples, pick them just before they reach full ripeness, discard (or eat straight away) any with blemishes or damage, wrap each in tissue paper and store separated from each other in a cool, dark spot.

How green is my citrus?

In some parts of Australia, notably the tropics, some citrus can be fully green and fully ripe. This is due to the warm overnight temperatures. In cooler zones and inland areas, citrus fruits develop their best flavour and colour when there's at least a 10°C difference between the day's maximum and minimum temperatures. In the tropics, the warm overnight temperatures affect the skin colour, and fruits can both be fully green while still being fully ripe. Even further south in Australia, if you leave fully ripe citrus on the tree during a warm spell, the fruit can revert to a green colour. It's perfectly edible, but it just doesn't look right.

Banana in a bag—it works!

It's true, if you seal a green, unripe fruit in a paper bag with a ripe banana will speed up the ripening process. Gases released by the ripe banana help to ripen up the fruit.

In season fruit and vegies

There will be many local variations in what's in season in your climate zone, but the following pages give a good all-round guide to what's likely to be cheapest, freshest and best-tasting in your shops, and for all the backyard farmers, in your own kitchen garden.

January

- Avocados
- Beans
- Blueberries, raspberries, strawberries
- Capsicum
- Cucumbers
- Grapes
- Limes
- Mango
- Oranges–Valencias
- Passionfruit
- Pears
- Stone fruit–apricot, nectarine, peach, blood plums
- Tomatoes
- Watermelons
- Zucchini

Yellow capsicums.

Pears.

February

- Avocados
- Beans
- Blueberries, raspberries, strawberries
- Capsicum
- Chillies
- Cucumbers
- Figs
- Grapes
- Limes
- Mango
- Oranges–Valencias
- Passionfruit
- Pears
- Stone fruit–apricot, nectarine, peach, plums
- Tomatoes
- Watermelons
- Zucchini

Left: Strawberries.

Right: Zucchini.

March

- Apples
- Beans
- Capsicums
- Cucumber
- Figs
- Ginger
- Grapes
- Limes
- Oranges–Valencias
- Passionfruit
- Pawpaw
- Pears
- Plums
- Pumpkin
- Quince
- Tomato
- Zucchini

Right: Apples.

Left: Pumpkins.

April

- Apples
- Avocado
- Beans
- Cabbage
- Capsicum
- Ginger
- Leek
- Limes
- Mandarin
- Pears
- Passionfruit
- Persimmon
- Pumpkin
- Quince

CHAPTER 8 *If you pick it, it will never get better*

Ginger.

Persimmon.

May

- Apples
- Avocado
- Broccoli
- Cabbage
- Chestnuts
- Ginger
- Leek
- Lemons
- Mandarin
- Oranges–Navel
- Pears
- Persimmon
- Quince
- Rhubarb
- Sweet potato

Broccoli.

Quince.

June

- Apples
- Avocado
- Beetroot
- Broccoli
- Cabbage
- Kiwifruit
- Leek
- Lemons
- Limes
- Mandarins
- Olives
- Onions
- Oranges–Navel
- Passionfruit–Panama
- Pears
- Pumpkin
- Quince
- Rhubarb
- Sweet potato

Beetroot.

Limes.

July

- Apples
- Avocados
- Beetroot
- Broccoli
- Cabbage
- Kiwifruit
- Leek
- Lemons
- Limes
- Mandarin
- Olives
- Onions
- Oranges–Navel
- Pumpkin
- Quince
- Rhubarb
- Sweet potato

Kiwifruit.

Mandarins.

August

Apples
Beetroot
Broccoli
Cabbage
Cumquat
Kiwifruit
Leek
Lemons
Mandarins
Onions
Oranges–Navel, Blood
Pumpkin
Rhubarb
Strawberries
Sweet potatoes

Lemons.

Rhubarb.

September

- Artichoke
- Beetroot
- Broad beans
- Broccoli
- Chillies
- Lemons
- Mandarin
- Oranges–Blood, Seville
- Pawpaw
- Strawberries

Artichoke.

Chillies.

October

- Artichoke
- Avocado
- Beetroot
- Broad beans
- Cucumber
- Chillies
- Grapefruit
- Passionfruit
- Pawpaw
- Zucchini

Left: Cucumber.

Right: Grapefruit.

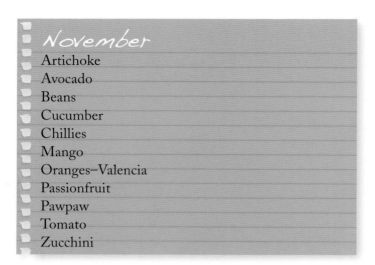

November

- Artichoke
- Avocado
- Beans
- Cucumber
- Chillies
- Mango
- Oranges–Valencia
- Passionfruit
- Pawpaw
- Tomato
- Zucchini

CHAPTER 8 *If you pick it, it will never get better*

Mangoes.

Passionfruit.

Right: Tomatoes.

December

- Apricots
- Beans
- Berries–black, blue, rasp and straw
- Capsicum
- Cucumber
- Mango
- Oranges–Valencia
- Passionfruit
- Pawpaw
- Stone fruit–nectarine, peach
- Tomato
- Zucchini

Left: Beans.

Right: Pawpaw.

CHAPTER 9
Dwarfs

*H*i ho, hi ho, it's off to work we go! (Trivia buffs might note that the Lone Ranger said Hi *Yo* Silver, not Hi *Ho* Silver.)

I love dwarfs. We live in the age of dwarfs: dwarf dogs (everything from Jack Russells to Maltese), dwarf cattle (Dexters, Lowlines, etc.), dwarf horses (Shetland ponies) and a vast range of dwarf plants.

As houses get bigger and bigger and blocks of land tend to shrink, there's no room for trees in backyards. Councils also introduced the tree preservation laws. In essence these laws dictate that you can't remove most trees unless you spend a fortune on arborists' reports and engineers' reports to prove the particular tree in question is a danger to civilisation as we know it.

So, if you plant a tree and it causes trouble, there will probably be nothing that you can do about it. And in any case, it could cost you thousands of dollars to repair the drive, the cracks in the house or the blockages in your pipes.

So, laws introduced to save trees have directly led to a total collapse in the numbers of trees being planted in backyards. No-one plants trees any more. Thus tree preservation laws have led to a huge decline in tree numbers in suburbia. Tree haters are still, legally or illegally, removing trees. But the tree lovers rarely plant them any more.

Hence the value of dwarfs. You can now get dwarf oranges, lemons, limes, mandarins, grapefruit, apples, pears, avocados, mangoes, peaches, nectarines, mulberries, figs…the list goes on and on. Dwarf fruit trees are generally so small that they classify as shrubs. They are usually no more than 2 or 3m tall. Thus, tree preservation laws don't apply to them.

Not only that:

- They still produce full-sized fruit.
- They are better than their big cousins in pots.
- In most cases they are exactly the same varieties as the big ones—eg. navel oranges, Granny Smith apples, etc.

But, best of all, you can fit a whole mini-orchard into a small backyard. Imagine your self-sufficiency backyard with chooks, dozens of herbs, vegies and fruit trees. A mini-farm with everything you need for survival: all grown organically.

So let's look at what is available:

Mini citrus

I'm quite sure that these will replace normal larger-sized citrus in gardens. The old oranges, mandarins, lemons etc grow about 3–5m (10–16ft) tall and 4m (13ft) or more wide. Dwarfs grow about 2m x 2m, yet they produce heaps of fruit.

The trick is that they discovered an understock called 'Flying Dragon'. This magical little plant provides the roots and they graft all the big varieties of fruit trees onto it. And, by magic, it stops the citrus from becoming too big. Where once you had one or two citrus, you can now have five or more.

A dwarf Valencia orange. Full-sized fruit on a miniature tree.

Almost every variety of citrus is now available in a dwarf form: Identical, but smaller.

Mini apples

As with the citrus, the trick here is usually a dwarfing understock. That is, the exact, same varieties grafted onto a special understock that keeps them small. Some mini apples are new varieties such as the Ballerina varieties which are small and narrow (like a pencil pine). You can fit a whole row of these in a small garden.

Mini peaches and nectarines

These glorious little babies only grow around 1 to 1.5m tall, yet their fruit are very big. Remember that peaches and nectarines (in fact most stone fruit) are troubled by fruit flies in many of the temperate to warmer zones. Since the law requires you to spray, don't buy peaches or nectarines if you are not willing to spray.

Mini avocados

Normal avocados grow bloody huge! They will easily fill up a small backyard. They are much too big for an average-sized garden. Dwarf varieties exist that grow around 2.5m (8ft) tall and still fruit their heads off. You need two to produce fruit, but any avocado in a neighbour's place within a block or two will do.

Mini figs

You can get white ones and black ones. They taste superb and are much lower maintenance since the bush is small enough to put mesh over it to keep out the birds. Nylon mesh is available at nurseries.

Mini mangoes

They grow about 2-4m (6.5–13ft) tall, probably only 2m in Sydney or Perth, taller up north. Don't forget to use a fungicide on the flowers or young fruit if the weather is rainy or humid in spring.

Mulberries

The big ones of these can fill one or two backyards. But then, the kids love them. They can climb them, eat the fruit and feed the silkworms. The new dwarf varieties only grow 2-4m (6.5–13ft) tall.

There are so many more dwarf fruit trees. Two mail-order nurseries have a huge range of these trees: Daley's Fruit Tree Nursery www.daleysfruit.com.au and Kendall Farms www.kendallfarms.com.au; ph 07 4779 1189

Other dwarf plants

All dwarfs are good—even Grumpy and Sneezy. Plant breeders have selected many dwarf flowering plants that are super garden specimens. Here follows a few:

- *Pittosporum tobira* 'Miss Muffet': This is a wonderful, rounded, low bush to 1m with perfumed white flowers. It is very dense, salt tolerant and very hardy.

- *Melaleuca hypericifolia* 'Ulladulla Beacon': I really love this ugly duckling. It grows into a super-dense low, rounded plant to about 50cm (20in) tall and produces bright red bottlebrush flowers. It is tolerant of salt spray, dry spots, wet spots, poor soil—the lot. It's only ugly while it's a baby.
- *Banksia integrifolia* prostrate: This grows to about 40cm (16in) tall and is very dense. The flowers are a greenish-yellow colour and it is very, very hardy.
- *Acmena* 'Allyn Magic': This is the best of the dwarf lillypillies. It grows around 1m (3ft) tall and is very hardy and dense.
- *Nandina domestica* 'Gulf Stream': This is a mile better than the older dwarf nandina called 'Nana'. It grows less than 1m tall and has superb foliage colour.

Check to see if any of these are good in your area.

The Dream

This is our dwarf fruit tree makeover from *Burke's Backyard*. This is a tiny backyard and now it has the lot.

We all dream of having the backyard with everything: areas to sit and have dinner, areas for the kids to play, artistic yet practical garden lighting, a clothes-drying area, lots of flowering plants, a barbecue area, a shaded area to sit under in summer and, perhaps most of all,

a fruit tree orchard that produces masses of fruit for the family.

But then it would also be good to have a garden shed, some lawn, lots of herbs and perfumed-leaved plants, plus a sandpit, a daybed and really lovely colours on the fence, paving

The garden before the makeover.

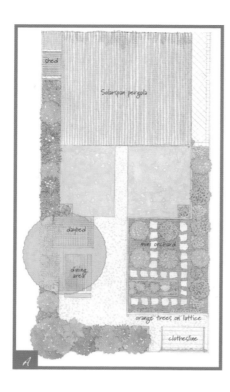

A: The garden plan. Illustration by Pamela Horsnell.

B: The passionfruit vine winds its way up the lattice.

and seating. That is what we built into our mini-orchard makeover: the bloody lot. All into a small backyard of a semi-detached home, measuring 11m x 8.5m.

It took three days to build the garden, during pouring rain. It would have taken two fine days. We have included the design to show you how easy it was to construct. The day bed doubles as a sandpit: remove the three wooden panels on top and the sandpit is underneath.

The service area is up the back, left-hand side. Even here there is a passionfruit vine on the fence next to a foldout clothesline.

The service area is hidden by the latticework to which is attached two espaliered navel oranges. Orange trees that are only 75mm thick!

The Sir Walter buffalo lawn area is for kids to play on and the decomposed granite/white gravel paving mix is more for the adults. It supports the dining table and chairs and provides access to everything.

A: The espaliered Navel oranges look great, provide privacy and lots of fruit. Best of all they are only three inches thick!

B: The huge loquat tree supports the gorgeous 12-volt outdoor lighting system.

Towering over the garden is a gigantic loquat tree. This produces superb orange-coloured fruit, but it also supports a 12-volt lighting system. We fitted 12 volt compact fluorescent lights into Telbix drop suspension lantern fittings with Dino glass from Cosmo Lighting in Kensington, Sydney (around $50 each. Ph 02 9662 1517).

Then we placed that whole assembly inside Wooden/Bamboo Shades from Shanghaied in Melbourne (03 9384 7888). They'll tell you of the nearest retailer in your state. These were between $90 and $190 each.

We also installed a Clipsal C-Bus Wireless Remote and Plug–adaptors to allow the lights to be turned on by a remote controller.

Since they're only 12 volts, it is totally safe and legal for any homeowner to install the light fittings. Our electrician ran a 240-volt line along the fence to an outdoor power point on the fence. We plugged a 12-volt transformer into the power point and ran the

12-volt cable up the loquat tree so the lights hang from the tree branches. The effect was excellent.

We removed the existing garden shed which dominated the entire backyard and replaced it with a slimline shed beside the house. We removed the acrylic panels from the pergola and replaced them with Solarspan panels that are made of two layers of Colorbond steel separated by polyurethane foam plastic. This gives extraordinary thermal insulation: an oasis in summer, away from the scorching heat.

The garden beds are all edged with ACQ treated pine railway sleepers: safe for the whole family. The sleepers and the fences were all painted with Taubman's Rialto exterior low sheen acrylic–a lovely mushroom colour that highlights foliage really well.

But the mini orchard! What a triumph! We fitted in:

- A Kaffir lime (in a pot)
- A dwarf Meyer lemon
- A dwarf Emperor mandarin
- A dwarf Tahitian lime
- A dwarf Valencia orange
- Two espaliered navel oranges
- A dwarf apple-tree
- A dwarf fig tree
- A dwarf mulberry tree
- A dwarf mango tree
- An enormous Loquat overhead
- Plus a large avocado hanging over the fence from next door.

A: The fences and sleepers were painted with Taubmans Rialto exterior low sheen acrylic.

B: A dwarf Meyer lemon.

C: A dwarf fig tree.

D: A dwarf mango tree.

A: Fourteen fruit trees in one tiny backyard plus 30 herbs, a dining area, sandpit, clothesline and a lawn!

B: AND a lovely undercover area protected by a Solarspan roof to admire the garden from.

Fourteen fruit trees in one backyard, plus a passionfruit vine, 30 assorted herbs including mints, basil, pineapple sage, coriander, parsley, oregano, sage, rosemary, thyme, and aloe vera.

All of this in a backyard that measures 11m x 8.5m (36ft x 28ft).

The owners Mick and Helen (and their 19-month-old toddler Isabella) celebrated a relative's 40th birthday, entertaining 16 people with a barbecue (herbs from the garden were used). They were still able to kick the footy around and have a bit of cricket.

Isabella loves her sandpit.

Everyone wins.

Isabella LOVES her sandpit.

CHAPTER 10
The wonderful world of manures

In a world without poo, all the flies would not breed
and soil would begin to run down
But a pile of manure is all that you need
Salvation with pong but don't frown

If you go to the country, and load up your boot
with chook poo and cow poo plus horse
You'll have garden success, and you'll save lots of loot
in growing organic of course

'It's the smell', I can tell, that your family will yell
'We fear it will injure the brain'
Good health is the issue with poo, not the smell
So just use it again and again.

*P*etrol prices are high, inflation is creeping upwards, money is short. How on earth can we save a buck? Poo is the answer: it always is (only the question ever changes). Chooks, pigs, sheep, cows, ducks and horses strain to extrude faecal perfection for us all. Horses produce wondrous scones of delight for our gardens. But sheep pellets, chook guano, cow pats, duck dollops and pig turds all have their place—hopefully not on the underside of your shoe though.

When you are on a trip into the country—to pick up fresh apple pies from a roadside stall—why not stop at the other stalls with spectacular bags of humming manure. Often as little as $1 or $2 will buy you a bag of fresh country manure. As you wend your way home you will be engulfed by the subtle fruity aroma from the apple pies plus the complementary sweet nutty waft from the pig turds. A bag of cow pats will hum along with the drone of your tyres while yielding yet another heady aroma. Doubtless all of those in the car will happily sing along. 'Old McDonald had a farm, ee-i-ee-i-oh—with a pig turd here and a cow pat there, ee-i-ee-i-oh'.

Of all of Mother Nature's gifts, none can surpass the humble horse scone. It is deeply distressing to me that this is such an outcast from the horticultural scene. Yes, I realise that crumbling cow pats by hand onto the camellias is one of life's precious experiences. I understand that scattering chook poo to the four winds as you dance through your garden is invigorating and delicious. But they throw most of the horse scones and stable manure away! Ye Gods, the world has gone mad!

Horse scones

Horses, such majestic creatures and creators of wonderful manure!

All right, I know horse manure has a bad name. But only amongst the dull and ignorant. Yes, it does happen that some stable manure sends up a green crop of wheat, barley or oats. This is a one-off event called a green manure crop. When the crop reaches around 30cm tall, pull it up and lay it on top of the ground. This is a real added bonus to the superb organic benefits of the manure itself as the green manure crop breaks down rapidly and never re-emerges.

Stable manure also contains wood shavings and/or hay. This too is superb as a soil conditioner. The urine (a free added extra!) helps break down the shavings or hay to produce organic colloids that will make any soil perfect.

One reason horse poo is so misunderstood is that some people have used it incorrectly. No manures should be used fresh; they should be aged, or more correctly, composted. Some people have used fresh stable manure, with sawdust or straw, and have noticed that their plants went a bit yellow. This means the manure was too fresh—not composted enough. As manure and organic matter break down, they use up nitrogen causing yellowing of the plants that then run short of nitrogen. But if you wait til it has composted for a few weeks, the manure releases nitrogen, producing strong, green growth in all plants.

So for goodness sake, if your manure is still in dry scones and not composted—wet it and wait a few weeks before using it.

Since horse manure is so poorly understood, you can usually get it free from larger horse stables. Often, they will let you load up a trailer load for free: this is about $85 worth of organic soil conditioner (ie. 1.5 cubic metres) for nix, nothing, gratis, nil, on the house, on the horse, without charge, at no cost!

All of my vegie gardens and fruit tree areas were made of a useless sandy soil with many trailer loads of stable manure added. Remember, the weeds in it don't come back—they are a once-only event. Of course, if the manure is properly composted at high temperatures you don't even get the weeds. My vegie and fruit tree gardens are very productive. God bless useful horses and dumb gardeners who leave the horse poo free for me.

Thus horse manure stands out as by the far the best manure for soil improvement around. It is usually very cheap or free and it is readily available around horse stables. Horse manure is not as strong a fertiliser as chook, cow or pig poo—but it is the best organic additive for soils.

Cow manure

What wonderful stuff. Neither the strongest nor the weakest manure as a fertiliser, beloved of azaleas, camellias and almost everything else. All of that and the cowpats make great Frisbees too!

No-one understands true bucolic joy until they have danced around a paddock picking up the pats then crumbling them by hand onto the garden. Adventurous souls will make a compost salad: part horse manure, part cow manure, part chook poo. Or an enriched compost with compost from the compost bin, enriched with cow, chook and horse.

Cows, milk, meat and manure. Who could ask for more?

Chook poo

Chook poo, pure organic gold.

This is the real deal, the duck's guts–it even smells like a fertiliser should smell. The wondrous health-giving ammoniacal gas is excellent for clearing the nose too. But as a fertiliser it is strong: like Peck's Paste, a little bit goes such a long way. Plain Dynamic Lifter is 100 per cent pure composted chook poo. Pure organic gold. Almost all garden plants love it in small doses (a handful to the square metre–perhaps half of that for natives). Citrus, roses, lawns, fruit trees and hibiscus adore the stuff–almost as much as I do. I'd use it as a deodorant if women were more understanding.

The new Dynamic Lifter for Fruit & Citrus is even better for the above plants as well as for leaf vegies.

The ridgy-didge gardener makes a horticultural tea from chook poo; here follows the time-honoured secret Burke family formula that dates back to my great grandfather (x 16 generations ago), Culpability Burke, a noted chicken thief in Tipperary Ireland.

Steep three buckets full of steaming chook poo in a garbage bin (not a Sulo) three-quarters full of water. Wait about a week, stirring daily. Decant the garden tea and dilute it with three parts of water and use it as a liquid fertiliser for most plants (except natives, orchids and bromeliads). Any remaining sludge can be sloshed on the garden or added to your compost bin.

Keep dry chook poo 30cm (12in) back from the trunks of all plants.

In areas of limestone soil (bits of Western Australia and South Australia especially), it may be better to use cow or horse manure to avoid lime overload.

Pig manure

This stuff even looks like poo. Its rich nutty, wheaten aroma is, once tried, never forgotten. Years after pig farmers sell their utes, you can still tell that the previous owners had pigs. It's a good slow-acting fertiliser for all plants, but it is hard to get since no-one will bag it up or deliver it to nurseries. Plants grow faster on pig manure in an attempt to get away from the smell: hence the phrase 'grow like stink'.

Sheep, llama and alpaca nuggets

Quite useful stuff. Nicely packaged as rounded nuggets, not overly strong, but usually only available in country areas: come to think of it, to quote the song...Any Poo will Doo. Use this stuff on most plants, a couple of handfuls per square metre.

Dog and cat droppings

With dog and cat waste, always wear gloves and bury it in the garden. It's good for the soil but keep it away from the compost bin.

But why manure?

Chemical fertilisers work very well. Most are scientifically formulated and contain an extraordinarily well-balanced mix of nutrients. But, they are rather unkind to the soil and maybe to you. Chemical fertilisers look like bags of salt because most of them are salts. Many are quite acidic, and over time this can lead to acid soils.

If you are using these artificial fertilisers, you should check your pH (acidity) of the soil every year. If it drops below 6.5, it's time to apply garden lime or dolomite to your soil. The really nasty fertiliser for causing soil acidity is sulphate of ammonia.

For much of the last century, each year the average lawn fanatic would top-dress the lawn and fertilise it with sulphate of ammonia. Both are bad practice…I feel a parable coming on–actually this is a true story.

A bloke brought in some sick bits of camellia to the nursery. 'Bloody things went yellow,' he said. 'Must need some acid stuff– camellias like acid soils.'

So Ignorant Don, the nurseryman, asked the usual questions:

- How often do you water the camellias?
- What do you fertilise them with?
- What sort of soil do you have?

All to no avail. Silly old Don couldn't work out what was wrong. Ignorant people these nursery people. The bloke said everything he did for the plant was perfect. So I asked me to bring me a sample of soil from around the camellias. 'I just want some bloody acid stuff,' he said. 'Bring me the soil first,' I said.

To cut to the chase, he eventually came in with some soil samples. They had a pH of 3! Since the pH scale is a logarithmic base 10 scale, and 7 is neutral, that means that the soil was 10,000 times too acidic. I turned into a prosecution lawyer and harried him with questions, but everything he did was (he claimed) perfect. So I asked, 'What do you do with the lawn?'. 'I love my lawn, I care for it meticulously–every year I fertilise with sulphate of ammonia.' Bingo! 'I'll bet the camellias are below the lawn area,' I said. 'How'd you know that?' he replied. The acidity from the lawn was washing downhill onto the camellia garden. Hence the pH of 3.

After a hearty argument I convinced him to lime his camellias which he was very uncomfortable with. Six months later he came in and I asked him: 'How are your camellias?' 'They're fine–lush and green and growing; must have just been some temporary thing.'

Artificial or synthetic or chemical fertilisers—call them what you like—are quite tough on the soil ecosystem. They can kill worms and generally upset the balance of microorganisms that live in the soil. They can change the pH and they may contain heavy metals or other nasty by-products of chemical manufacture.

Manures, for the most part, tend to be free of nasty chemicals, don't drastically alter the soil acidity and they are spectacularly good for soil ecosystems. They lead to increased worm and dung-beetle activity. These hard working animals vigorously tunnel through the soil, aerating and adding organic matter deep down in the soil profile. Over time, worms and dung beetles will totally transform soils, increasing the soil's performance many times over. And silly people keep the worms in worm farms!

Lastly, manures improve soil structure which is essential for the soil to work properly. And silly people wash or park their cars on the lawn, which destroys the soil structure more or less permanently. One after lastly; manures are much healthier fertilisers to use in the vegie garden. This way you will produce organic vegies that minimise the toxic load of nasty chemicals on your (and the kids') bodies.

Pedants note that some manures still do include traces of antibiotics (especially chook poo) and worming compounds (especially horse and cow poo) that were given to the animals for their health. Sunlight and composting tend to break these chemicals down pretty rapidly though.

Synthetic fertilisers

There are a number of different sorts of synthetic fertilisers.

1. Slow-release fertilisers (aka controlled-release fertilisers)
2. (a) Complete fertilisers
   (b) Specialist fertilisers
3. Liquid fertilisers

These are not plant 'foods'. Plants feed on sugar which they make from sunlight. Excess sugar is turned into starch (ie. plant fat). So if you want to feed your plants, give them sunlight.

To make sugars, plants do need fertilisers, although interestingly, Australian native plants don't need much fertiliser at all. Fertilisers are devilishly confusing because fertiliser companies want to sell you as many bags as they can. So let's look at the various types and then see, at the end, what you really need.

Slow (or controlled) release fertilisers

The Schapelle Corbys of fertilisers: they get released very slowly. Modern potting mixes are a mix of composted wood wastes and, perhaps, sand. That is, there is no *soil* in them. So scientists developed little slow-release capsules full of fertiliser that release a little bit every day when the days are warm and wet. These fertilisers do the thinking for you and make up for the fact there is no soil in the mix.

Curiously, while soil works well in the ground, it does not work at all well in a pot. It stays too wet and therefore lacks air in between the particles. Soil-less mixes are much better in pots.

Slow-release fertilisers such as Osmocote or Nutricote are so spectacularly good that almost all plants grown in nurseries in Australia are grown with these fertilisers. Without them, your plants are unlikely to do well in pots. There are two useful types: slow-release native plant foods and all the rest. Native plants, especially grevilleas, banksias, waratahs, hakeas and (non-native) proteas, will be poisoned by normal fertilisers. You must use special native types. For non-native plants, any type will do.

2 (a) Complete fertilisers

These are your general run-of-the-mill fertilisers that contain everything that plants need to grow. They are suitable for most plants, excepting those listed in Specialist fertilisers below. Brands such as Thrive Granular, Brunning's Complete Garden Food or even Dynamic Lifter Fruit & Citrus (in effect a complete fertiliser).

2 (b) Specialist fertilisers

You don't need many of these. Rose food is the same as Citrus food, so don't buy both. Special Native Plant Fertilisers on the other hand are essential. Azalea and Camellia food is not necessary: use some cow manure or any slow-release fertiliser every couple of years. Azaleas and camellias are not all that hungry for fertiliser. Come to think of it, very few plants are 'gross feeders' that is, plants that would demand lots of fertilisers.

Roses, citrus, hibiscus, fruit trees, vegies and lawns all love their fertiliser. Citrus food does all of those except lawns—get a slow-release lawn food such as Scotts Lawn Builder for your lawns. It's the only lawn fertiliser I know that is safe to use in the vicinity of native plants—but not too close!

Campbell's Orchid Fertilisers are excellent, but I use Nitrosol for all of my orchids, bromeliads, ferns and native plants. Dynamic Lifter Fruit & Citrus formulation is superb for all fruit and citrus (plus roses and hibiscus) and vegies.

It's absolutely critical to only use native plant fertilisers on Australian plants. General or strong fertilisers kill them.

Liquid fertilisers

Nitrosol is the best in my view. It's mostly organic and contains triacontanol, which is a good natural growth hormone. Aquasol and Thrive are inorganic fertilisers, but very good.

So, for a general garden you might limit yourself to:

- Nitrosol liquid feed
- Osmocote or Nutricote slow release
- Osmocote or Nutricote slow release for natives
- Dynamic Lifter for Fruit & Citrus or Citrus food
- Scotts Lawn Builder
- Dynamic Lifter (original formula)
- Plus Seasol, the root promoter and plant health promoter (not really a fertiliser)

CHAPTER II
R'cycling and the 'Nvirament

We all want to help Planet Earth. We all know that doom is upon us and human life (and all else) will soon end.

Take Jamie and Jamie Connolly. They never married since Jamie is scared of commitment and Jamie is waiting for the perfect man to appear. They have three kids—McKenzie, Campbell and O'Brien. McKenzie went overseas this year, well actually she couldn't as the government wouldn't give her a passport since she didn't have a Christian name: only two surnames (her parents couldn't afford a Christian name since Kai, Jjon, Siiiimon and Jaycab—his kids from his two previous partners—cost so much in maintenance).

But they care about the 'nvirament. They have a worm farm, a water tank and a r'cycling bin and never use plastic supermarket bags. They know that by 2018 all life on earth will be extinct, so Jamie is expecting her new baby in a few weeks since you get the baby bonus. She plans to send this to Pamper the Pandas. It's a not-for-profit group because the CEO and staff pay themselves really well.

Campbell doesn't have a Christian name either, but he works at Camel's Breath Café and sends half his pay to Greenwar to fund its fight to save overpopulated whales in Antartica (since they look like his customers). Maybe if he could borrow a spare 'i' from Siiiimon, he could bend it into a c to add into Antarctica.

Each year the whole family participates in Greenup Australia. On that day they all plant a tree. The tree they planted last year died, but they are happy that they felt so good on the day. The tree was Acacia pycnantha and it is now declared a noxious weed in their area anyway. This makes Australia the only country on earth that has labelled its floral emblem a weed.

Last year Jamie asked Jamie to pipe the greywater onto the garden since they believe water isn't a renewable resource. The garden is now dead but obviously the environment is benefitting and this is a small price to pay.

They also put solar panels on the roof, but the man next door planted a row of Leighton Green cypress which now shade out all of the sun. They offset all of this by purchasing carbon credits from a local chimneysweeper.

Problem solved. Now environmentalists, you can skip the rest of this chapter as you know it all anyway. See ya!

Have they gone? Good. Let's crunch some science.

1. Plastic supermarket bags are not an environmental problem. Environment groups were misleading when they said these bags were killing many sea creatures, etc. In landfill in Australia they are also not a problem. They don't break down rapidly, but neither does anything else as the systems are sealed to prevent runoff of leachates (toxic stuff).

2. Minke whales are okay for the Japanese to harvest, according to Dr Tim Flannery and others. This can be sustainable activity if done well. Focusing on saving big or cute animals is not good for the environment: we need a less manipulative approach.

3. Recycling aluminium cans is a good idea, but it has happened more or less since day one of manufacture. Glass, paper and plastic are dubious things to recycle, probably doing little for the environment. The first five years or more of paper recycling saw it mostly dumped as landfill–but no-one admitted it.

4. Water tanks less than 10,000 litres are of dubious value. A small garden (excluding the lawn) uses around 2500 litres of water for a single watering. Thus even a 10,000-litre tank only does four waterings. At one every fortnight, that's still only eight weeks of happy plants.

5. Worm farms are made of plastic and have no environmental value at all. Better to breed worms in a compost heap and in garden soil by adding lots of organic matter.

6. Feel-good once-a-year days will never save the planet. One-day tree plantings, etc. are just feel-good exercises. Could they be set up to increase revenue for some group wanting money or power?

7. Greywater is fairly nasty stuff. Over a number of years of use, salt, sodium and phosphorus tend to accumulate in your soil. The constant wetness and these chemicals tend to kill off local native plants and garden plants but they also tend to favour certain weeds such as lantana, privet, asparagus weed and many others.

8. Solar roof panels have some value, but they are a very poor choice compared to clean efficient power generation in large power stations. Again, they are feel-good activities.

There are many things you can do that will help the environment: the world is not going to die. The real problems are governments that made awful mistakes like building ever-larger populations in cities like Sydney and Melbourne, without providing extra water for the new populations. Australia has always had droughts and, up to 1960, our governments constructed water-collection systems to cover the droughts. Over the past 50 years they simply didn't bother. They purchased land around the cities zoned rural, re-zoned these areas residential and sold the land off in blocks to you guys, making billions. Yet they failed to spend any significant amount of it to provide extra water for the mugs who bought the land.

The real problem is abysmal city planning. We need to grow new populations in attractive areas where there are good jobs, good schools, good restaurants, good cinemas–and access to water. Decentralisation didn't work as you can't take people into the wilderness (ask Moses). But smart regional planning will work.

So governments are keeping you guys busy with tokenistic activities, hoping you won't work out how they stuffed up.

Some environmental groups appear to be just people wanting power and money, colluding with government to keep you confused and breathless. Together, they fiddle while Rome burns.

What you can do to help

Most of the rainwater that falls on your suburban block is wasted, as you'll see in the diagram in the next chapter. It falls on the roof, paving or driveway then it is chanelled into pipes and off to wreck the local creek. Water tanks collect a small portion of the water from one or two downpipes only. You can double your rainfall (sometimes you can increase it up to 10 times) by using the water from the roof for your garden. Just cut off the downpipes and re-divert the water out onto the lawn or into the garden. Even if the downpipe goes into a tank, direct the overflow (the vast majority of the water) out into the garden. You could also use the Atlantis system, which is plastic milk crate-like material that allows the excess rainwater to soak into your soil. This is a modern equivalent of the old rubble pit or rubble drain. www. atlantiscorp.com.au.

You can also pave areas such that the runoff soaks into a garden area. Some paving such as decomposed granite lets water soak into the

A: Cut off your downpipes and divert water out onto the lawn or into the garden.

B: The Atlantis system uses plastic milk crate-like material to allow excess water to soak into your soil. For more on how this system works, see Chapter 12.

ground below, as do concrete pavers if gaps are left.

By the way, never wash or park your car on the lawn. This will crush the soil, permanently damaging the lawn and nearby shrubs and trees.

There are more rainbow lorikeets now than in 1770 when Jim Cook arrived.

Birds

There are far more rainbow lorikeets now than when Jim Cook arrived in 1770. They used to fly up and down the east coast of Australia chasing the flowering gum trees. Now, domestic gardens are so nectar-rich that the lorikeets are sedentary, breeding birds in all areas on the east coast.

What you can do in your garden has a huge impact on local bird populations:

- Do put out seed for finches and parrots. This enables them to survive in areas where their seeding grasses, etc. have been killed or mown, while they learn to adapt to suburban life (as sparrows and pigeons have done already).
- Do plant grevilleas, bottlebrushes, banksias, kangaroo paws, gum trees, sasanqua camellias, mahonias and any other plants that feed local birds.
- Do lay out your garden with narrow lawn areas to repel foreign birds but attract native ones.
- Do put out water dishes for your birds. Put a rock or two in them to prevent drowning.

A: Do put out seed for finches and parrots.

B: Do plant trees and shrubs that feed native birds such as banksias (pictured), as well as grevilleas, bottlebrush, kangaroo paws, mahonias, sasanqua camellias and gum trees.

C: Do put out water dishes for your birds. Putting a few rocks in the middle can save birds from drowning.

Plants

Local native plants (ie. indigenous ones) are really important. Protect any surviving local plants—not just gum trees. It is silly just to preserve trees—we need grasses, shrubs and climbers too. Perhaps there is a local indigenous nursery in your area that sells local plants (ask at your local nursery). Even just one or two indigenous plants will do. This helps protect marsupials, birds, lizards and hosts of other local animals.

Kids can easily propagate native gum trees from seed. Just grab some seed capsules from the tree and put them in a paper bag. In a week you should have loads of very fine reddish-brown seeds that can be grown in pots of potting mix then planted out.

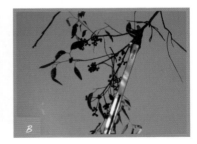

A + B: Collecting gum seeds is a great one for the family. Collect some seed capsules from a gum tree.

A + B: The kids can put them in a paper bag and set it aside for a week or so.

C: Soon they'll have seeds ready to plant.

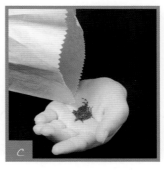

Re-using

Use it up, wear it out, make it do or do without. That's my motto. An old wooden box can be used for storage in the garage or to grow vegies in. An old tricycle can be repaired and repainted for your younger child.

Re-use old rags in the garage or tool shed. Re-use old plastic supermarket bags for rubbish disposal or a thousand other things. Get a bench grinder and re-point old, blunt screwdrivers.

Re-use everything you can. These old wooden boxes were perfect for growing strawberries, Asian vegies and herbs in. To find out how, see Chapter 7.

Tool maintenance

Coat wooden handled tools (spades, rakes, brooms, etc) with 50/50 linseed oil and mineral turpentine each year—this will add years to their life and save your hands from splinters. Oil all your metal tools—saws, secateurs, snips, pliers, etc. on wet days when you can't work outside.

Re-use plastic plant pots.

A: Look after your tools and they'll last a lifetime. Coat all wooden handles with a 50/50 mix of linseed oil and mineral turps each year.

B: Re-use your plastic pots.

Do compost all kitchen scraps, plus prunings, non-bulbous weeds, dead leaves, and lawn clippings. Never allow green waste to leave your property.

Do procure all the animal poo that is discarded in your neighbourhood. Never throw out old soil. Local or site soil is always better than what you can buy. Add a good quality coarse sand and compost to your soil and use it again and again.

Eat in, not out. Entertain at home.

Holiday at home—or at least in Australia.

For those who want to make Australia a better place, why not create a native bird sanctuary.

You'd be surprised how much control you can have over which birds enter your garden, and which ones don't, just by the way you go about laying it out, then planting it. Try my sample design on for size on page 202.

You've heard of horse whisperers—the people who know how horses think? Well, gardeners can become bird whisperers if they spend a bit of time learning how birds think and behave. You can strongly influence which birds visit your garden, and which ones fly away, with your garden layout and choice of plantings.

Now, we all know which birds everyone wants to see the back of: Indian mynahs. These exotic pests gang up on other birds and chase them away. They're fearless—they'll even take on much larger birds like king parrots and white cockatoos and see them off. And they do this because they're smart. Indian mynahs aren't likeable, but in a way you've got to admire them.

It wasn't their fault that people imported them to Australia to control insects on cane plantations back in the 1880s. (Now, feral pests introduced to help out cane farmers, where else have I heard that story?). It would be stretching things to call Indian mynahs 'flying cane toads' but these birds do make life very tough for many native bird species. However it is possible to discourage them from your garden.

Before we get onto how that's done, Indian mynahs aren't the only undesirable pest birds, and it's not just exotic birds which bully native birds. Native noisy miners and their close relatives, the bellbirds, will drive almost every other bird species from their territory. When you hear the tinkling call of bellbirds in the bush, you know you're in a sick, sad forest of ailing gum trees that's devoid of most other bird species. And watch wattlebirds at work—they're very aggressive towards any other birds which try to feed on 'their' nectar plants.

Then there are the home-owners who actually side with the flying bullies. These are usually kindly, nature-loving people who don't realise they're doing the wrong thing by feeding carnivores such as visiting magpies, butcher birds and kookaburras. They toss out bits of meat that get snapped up, but does that satisfy the hunger of the carnivores? Not likely. That just gives them energy to hunt for small bird species such as blue wrens, silvereyes and finches. In many parts of Australia, the populations of carnivores such as magpies, kookaburras, currawongs, crows, ravens and butcher birds is out of control. Feeding these birds only makes things worse.

Even though that's a pretty grim picture I paint, there is still a lot you can do in your own backyard to change things around. For starters, stop feeding the carnivores meat. But after you've weaned yourself off that habit, get out in your garden, change a few plantings here and there and you can make the world of difference. Here's what to do.

Fair go

Getting things back in balance, so the smaller, gentler native bird species get a fair go at enjoying some food and shelter, requires a few changes in what you grow, plus a change of layout here and there. This is where you become a bird whisperer.

Here's a handy fact: feral pests such as Indian mynahs, sparrows, turtledoves, feral pigeons and starlings, plus our own native pest bird, the noisy miner, all love open, grassy or paved areas dotted with trees (and that's why you find them taking over your local parks, too). These birds hate densely planted shrubberies—they want the wide open spaces that lawns provide.

And here's a handy solution: crowd them out with plants, break up their wide open spaces. They'll hate it when you replace some of the lawn with shrubs and other plantings. The second step is to plant bird-attracting plants that offer food as well as shelter to bring the native birds back.

It works

I know that changing your plantings has a huge effect on the birds which visit because I've been doing this in my gardens for the past 35 years.

Grevillea 'Robyn Gordon'.

In my first garden, in Chatswood in Sydney, I planted the wonderful long-flowering *Grevillea* 'Robyn Gordon' plus many other grevilleas, banksias and kangaroo paws. This provides a steady stream of nectar year round, and each year we saw an increase in the number of species visiting. In the first year after planting the 'Robyn Gordons', etc. we saw, for the first time, white-cheeked honeyeaters, silvereyes, blue wrens and eastern spinebills. Probably the major single benefit of planting 'Robyn Gordon' is that it flowers it winter. For the local native birds, winter can be a tough time and many actually starve to death. But with 'Robyn Gordon' and banksias planted in numbers, they survive and thrive.

When we first moved into my current property out on Sydney's north-western fringe, most of it was bare, open and filled with pest bird species. Now we have around 200 species of native birds visiting, and very few feral pest species. There are noisy miners in the district, but not in our garden.

We do occasionally get visited by non-native turtledoves, but they're usually in company with native bronzewing pigeons, white-headed pigeons, brown pigeons, wonga pigeons, crested pigeons, diamond doves, bar-shouldered doves and peaceful doves, so they're in some classy company when we see them.

We still have lawns here, but they are long, narrow and winding, not broad and open. And we have planted plenty of 'Robyn Gordon' grevilleas as well, plus I've made sure that winter food stocks are plentiful with banksias, grevilleas, wattles and many other winter-flowering native species planted here.

Design details

Of course, most people won't fill up their gardens so they're chocker with plants, just to attract native birds. Everyone has land rights–birds, bees, kids and even home-owners! So, how do you strike the balance so you help out the native birds, but keep some good, usable space for your family?

The garden plan we show here includes all the essential elements that could be included in a bird-friendly garden design. Feel free to adapt it to your backyard, and your way of living.

The main thing is to break up the single, wide open space of a wide lawn and instead create a series of useful 'garden rooms'. One 'room' might be for the kids to play in, another for you hang out the washing,

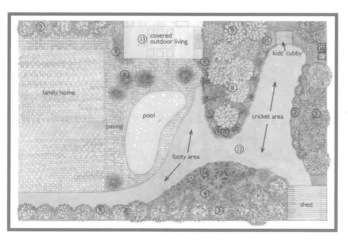

Bird-friendly garden design plan. Garden plan illustration by Pamela Horsnell.

another for growing vegies, and another an entertainment area for everyone to sit around a table and take it easy on weekends. You could separate each area with garden beds, shrubs, screens or even a frog pond. Try to avoid big expanses of paving–they're hot in summer and very wildlife-unfriendly at all times.

Plantings

You occasionally hear so-called experts advising people to plant small, spiky, short-flowering native shrubs in their gardens. This is nonsense, and most people wouldn't do that anyway. It doesn't look good. Besides, there are many small, beautiful, bird-friendly, flowering native plants for gardeners to choose from, so there's no reason to include any ugly plants in your bird-friendly garden.

See our listing here of the main plantings used in this design. All either flower well or produce excellent foliage. They include bottlebrushes, kangaroo paws, grevilleas, banksias, Gymea lilies, grass trees and seeding weeds which all feed wild birds.

Major plantings

1. Mixed bottlebrushes: *Callistemon* 'Harkness'; *C.* 'Captain Cook'; *C.* 'Hannah Ray'
2. *Baeckea virgata* 'Miniature'
3. *Syzygium francisii* 'Little Gem'
4. Gymea lily (*Doryanthes excelsa*)
5. *Austromyrtus inophloia*
6. Potted grass trees
7. *Lomandra longifolia* 'Tanika'
8. Tropical grevilleas–*Grevillea* 'Robyn Gordon'; *G.* 'Honey Gem'; *G.* 'Golden Lyre'; *G.* 'Flamingo'; *G.* 'Pink Surprise'.
9. Mixed banksias–*Banksia spinulosa*, *B. serrata*, *B.* 'Hinchinbrook'
10. Kangaroo paws
11. Bird grasses (weeds for seeds), *Panicum maximum* (Guinea grass), *Ehrharta erecta* (panic veldt grass).

And if you have any other ideas, please email them to us at thelazygardener@burkesbackyard.com.au

Syzygium francisii 'Little Gem'.

The outstanding privacy plant, *Syzygium francisii* 'Little Gem', grows well everywhere, except in our coldest areas. It reaches around 2.5m (8ft) tall and wide, is very dense, looks superb and hardly, if ever, needs pruning. Be warned though, it's not all that dense or attractive as a young pot plant.

'Little Gem' and the miniature baeckeas are superb nesting plants for birds–very dense with lots of forks for nests. Neither are prickly.

The *Austromyrtus inophloia* down the sides is a lilly pilly relative and very pretty. It loves part-shade.

Like the 'Robyn Gordon' grevillea, the autumn-winter flowering banksias (*B. spinulosa*, *B. ericifolia*, *B. serrata* and *B.* 'Hinchinbrook') will provide lots of food in winter.

Alternatives

Eucalyptus 'Summer Red'.

Visit a specialist native nursery, or check out local garden centres to see which ones have good stocks of native plants. Perhaps you won't be able to find one or two plants I mention here, or maybe they're not suited to your local climate. So you'll need to look for alternatives. That shouldn't be a problem. Good alternatives to look for include the small (5–7m tall) flowering gums such as 'Summer Red' and the pink 'Summer Beauty'. Paperbarks

A: Eucalyptus 'Summer Beauty'.

B: Queensland firewheel tree
   (Stenocarpus sinuatus).

(*Melaleuca* sp.) are worth trying, as is the stunning Queensland firewheel tree (*Stenocarpus sinuatus*). All attract and feed birds.

Growing natives

What's the best soil for growing natives? Crushed rock. Fabulously free-draining, it's the best stuff there is. I use crushed sandstone in my garden, and the excellent native plantings around the 2000 Olympic site at Homebush Bay in Sydney all grow in crushed sandstone.

When you think about it, this makes sense. Australia's bush soils are thin and low in nutrients, and most native plants in the wild grow in broken-down rock. In the garden, you can mix crushed rock in with your own soil, but I prefer to use it as a 300mm (12in) deep layer on top of the soil. Cover it with leaf litter mulch to finish it all off.

Crushed rock is the best soil for growing natives in. I used crushed sandstone in my garden.

Natives in the wild certainly won't live happily in the alluvial silts which many landscape companies sell. My advice is to avoid commercially available soils (especially in Sydney and Brisbane, where many landscapers' soils are sourced from alluvial silts). These soils have the consistency of glue and native plants won't thrive in them. And don't let them sell you 'washed' river sands, either. Most of them are terrible for growing any sorts of plants in, let alone natives.

In Sydney, crushed sandstone, which is what I use, is readily available. It's sometimes sold as sandstone roadbase. In Melbourne, another crushed rock, such as coarse blue metal mix, would be suitable. In Canberra, the people from Stonehenge in Pialligo (phone 02 6248 9063) have developed a good rubble mix for natives. And in Brisbane, look for crushed rock roadbase. In Perth, the crushed rock there is limestone, and that wouldn't be suitable for natives, but the Perth soil is sandy in most areas, so you've got it made.

If you can't find crushed rock in your area, one option is to stick with what you've got, even if it's clay. Far too many people take the supposedly 'easy' option, dig out a layer of clay soil, replace it with trucked-in alluvial soil from a landscaper—and their natives don't thrive. Despite its reputation for being like concrete, clay soils can be turned into very good soils, if you're patient. See Chapter 4 for more details on how to turn clay into good garden soil, but the magic words to remember are gypsum, compost and persistence.

Finally, the other smart option for growing native plants in areas with ordinary or poor soil drainage is to create raised garden beds. Raise the soil level 30cm or so higher than the surrounding soil, make sure the soil in the raised bed won't wash away in rain (ie. retain it with sleepers, or rocks, etc.) and plant into that.

Most native soils thrive on good soil drainage (bottlebrushes and melaleucas are an exception though, as they can cope with poorly drained soils quite well), so make a priority of improving soil drainage before you plant anything.

Fertilising and care

The other thing to know about growing native plants is that they don't like much fertiliser at all, and they might die if you give them the wrong stuff. But it's not hard to get it right. Just give them fertilisers which state 'formulated for native plants' on the package. There's usually a range of products suited to natives available in any good garden centre. They're not hard to find. The slow-release fertilisers for natives (eg. Osmocote) make it very easy to fertilise them, but various other types of fertilisers are available. Just make sure not to overdo it with the fertiliser. Stick to the packet directions.

The other thing that many native plants need to keep on looking good is regular pruning. Grevilleas and bottlebrushes will flower better, grow more densely and look better if you cut off the dead flower heads after they finish flowering. Without pruning, they can tend to become a bit straggly over time, so get out the shears after the flower show is over, just cut a bit off (remove up to one-third of the plant if you feel like, but you don't have to remove that much if you don't want to) and you'll be amazed how good they'll look in just a few weeks' time.

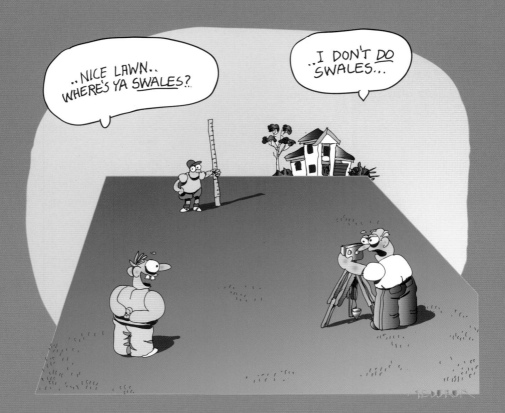

CHAPTER 12
The bloody lawn

*I*f there's a sign that typifies the 20th century, it's 'Keep Off The Grass'. Go to a park and the sign would scream at you. Go to Maurie's home and his lawn is just as sacred. After all, he's spent 40 years of his life perfecting his lawn. He used to offer kids $2 (a quid) for every weed they could find in his lawn. He never had to pay out because even the eagle-eyed kids couldn't spot a single weed.

Maurie loves his lawn more than he loves Gwen, his wife. Gwen's a good woman, but his lawn is sheer perfection. Every year he top-dresses and fertilises his lawn: he sprays all the weeds and no-one walks on his lawn…except Maurie, but even then it is only when he's guiding his mower or spraying the weeds.

But now, his grandson Hunter has told him his lawn is going to destroy the planet. Hunter reckons that the TV gardener Jason Oliver says lawns are really bad for the 'nvirament.

In the media, they have special names for everything, thus environment becomes 'nvirament (see Translators' Media Word Guide at the end of this chapter).

Jason Oliver says lawns use up far too much water and chemicals and we can't have them any more: we must pave everything, preferably in concrete pavers. So who's right–trendy Jason or stolid Maurie?

The truth is that both are victims of their times. Neither has thought through their actions. Poor old Maurie just did what everyone else did and there was nothing to indicate he was doing anything wrong. Jason is another opportunist making media mileage with trendy catch phrases.

My lawn is the best part of my garden's environmental design. For more than 25 years I have captured and used all the rain that falls on my block of land. My lawn does most of this for me.

About 75 per cent of the rainwater that falls on the average block goes off into the stormwater system. Rain that falls on the roof, paved areas and driveways is all diverted to stormwater drains. This water is wasted and wrecks the local creeks.

About 75 per cent of most blocks of land is paved. The driveway is paved, the patio is paved, the house itself is more or less a giant paver, as are the shed and any other outbuildings. Almost all of that water goes into drainage pipes, often via roof guttering. That is, 75 per cent of the rainfall from your block of land goes off into the stormwater system and wrecks the local creek. This is Jason's system and it is crazy and very bad for the environment. Even if you have water tanks, most of the water from those downpipes is lost via the overflow pipe. Water tanks fill rapidly when it rains, then the rest of the rain goes down the drain.

Back to my place. All of my captured rainwater (from the roof, paving, etc) is run onto the gardens and out onto the lawn areas. All that I did was to cut off my downpipes from the roof, and direct the water into the garden or out onto the lawns. My lawns are technically swales; they are grassy zones that direct the flow of water and slow it

A: I cut off my drainpipes from the roof and direct the water into the garden or out onto the lawns.

B: My lawns are technically swales. They direct the flow of water and slow it down so it can soak in.

C: Cross-section of the lawn swales.

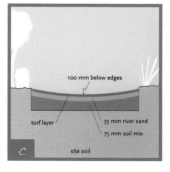

100 mm below edges

turf layer

35 mm river sand

75 mm soil mix

site soil

down to soak into the ground. My lawn areas are about 15cm higher at the sides than in the middle—so they act as shallow open drains.

All of my garden beds are slightly raised (from 20cm to 1.5m) to capture and direct rainwater runoff. The end result is that my rainwater is directed around the lawn and garden areas constantly zigzagging and slowing down so that it soaks into the soil. You can do this very subtly in your own garden. After 25 years of my garden having zigzags and swales, no-one has ever noticed. No one has said, 'Why is your lawn higher at the sides than in the middle?' They don't notice.

The plants do though. They grow like stink. But you can do better than me if you want to. My land has a few miserable centimetres of soil over solid rock, so I am very limited. The new Atlantis system—www.atlantiscorp.com.au—which you can bury in the ground (if you don't have rock like me) is awesome. It acts like the old rubble drains or rubble pits. You dig a hole in the ground, place the black plastic

Geotextile

Rainwater Harvesting Tank

A: The garden areas are constantly zigzagging, slowing down the water so it soaks into the soil.

B: The Atlantis system cross-section.

C: Dig a hole in the ground.

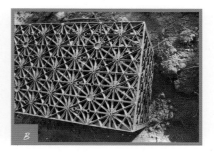

A + B: Put the black plastic milk-crate-like material in the hole.

C + D: Cover the crates with geotextile fabric and backfill the hole.

milk-crate like material inside, cover that with geotextile fabric and backfill with the soil. Then you simply run your water from your downpipes into the milk-crate stuff. It soaks into the ground and your plants will send roots in and suck it up. What they don't use goes down into the underground aquifers to top up your groundwater.

All of this is a one-off job and passive. It needs no pumps, no electricity, has no moving parts and is very cheap to buy. The soil that you get out of the hole in the ground can be used to create the raised garden beds and the raised edges to the lawn. Nothing is wasted.

Although water moves very little sideways through soils normally, it moves large distances sideways when under the sort of pressure that builds up in your underground pit. Thus shrubs, trees and the lawn are watered efficiently from below. Free water, not wasted water.

Don't over-fertilise the lawn either. Just use some slow-release lawn food such as Scotts Lawn Builder once every second spring.

So much for Jason's damaging the environment stuff. Be very careful who you listen to. There is only one true Messiah, but he always denies his divinity. For the record, I am not the Messiah.

So, have a lawn if you wish, it can be very good for the environment. For most middle to northern areas of Australia, one of the soft leaf buffalo lawns is a great choice. I love Sir Walter. It is drought and cold tolerant and needs little fertilising. It is also quite shade tolerant.

Most couch grasses won't tolerate the shade and therefore go bare and ratty around the shady edges of the lawn. For cooler zones, ryegrass, fescue and bent mixes are really good. But there are many other grass types, so you should seek local knowledge from neighbours, local gardening experts and also from local nurseries before you buy your lawn.

A: Sir Walter lawn.

B: Sir Walter turf being laid. Photos courtesy of Sir Walter Turf.

Mowing

Maurie slaughters his lawn. He mows it 2cm (1in) high. He is wrong. At racetracks they mow it around 10cm (4in) high and it looks beautiful. For home lawns this is too high. For most lawns mow it around 4cm (1.5in) tall and remember this: clean, sharp, well-cut lawn edges make even a third rate lawn look good.

Always spend time cutting the edges, it really pays off. I cut mine with a sharpened spade. You may care to lay a treated pine edge—use

A: Don't slaughter your lawn, put your mower up a notch and mow it around 4cm high.

B: Keeping the edges of your lawn cut looks fantastic, a sharp spade will do a great job.

75 x 25mm ACQ treated pine. This is a safer product than CCA treated pine (the older variety) but you may need to get your timber yard to order it in for you. You need in-ground rated ACQ timber too.

There are other edging materials available such as aluminium strips, bricks laid on a mortar base or whatever takes your fancy.

Mowers

Next time you need a new mower, get a four-stroke one. These are the same as your family car. That is, they have oil and petrol in separate tanks, not mixed together. A cheap two-stroke is 40 times more polluting per hour than a car and more than 20 times more polluting than a four-stroke mower. So get a four-stroke one.

Four-stroke mowers are far less polluting than two-stroke mowers. The four-stroke mowers have oil and petrol in separate tanks, just like your car.

Fake lawns

Lawns are still the highest maintenance part of any garden. The new varieties of fake grass are low maintenance and are very good indeed. They are a realistic alternative to living grass. Fake grass is a much better choice in heavy wear areas and in areas where the kids play cricket or basketball or where the adults play golf. Modern synthetic grass types last more than 10 years and are hard to pick from the real stuff.

If you lay them on compacted porous road base (eg. crushed sandstone) they can also absorb water for the soil beneath the base.

Why lawns?

Research has shown that most people want a garden or park to have grass, water and trees. These three elements resonate with us and create a relaxing environment.

A number of solid pieces of research have been done on people and landscapes. All of them have revealed that most people want a garden or park to be made up of grass, water and trees. These three things resonate with our psyche and create enjoyable, relaxing environments. Remember that our ancestors evolved in the African grasslands and then became coastal migrants.

- You need grass to relax on
- You need grass to play on
- You need grass to look at

For purists

- If you worry about even a four-stroke mower's pollution–buy a push mower. Soon you will be super fit.

- Equally, if you have paving, replace the blower with a straw broom.
- Use a mulching mower to push the grass clippings back into the soil to reduce the need for fertilisers.

Translators' Media Word Guide

A pedant's guide to translating media words into English. Note that an apostrophe means a neutral sound: so R'leaf = relief. Equally, in all words except vulnerable, the u is also neutral.

Word	Media take on it	Correct pronunciation
Australia	Oz <u>Tray</u> Lee Ya	Oz <u>Trail</u> Ya
Billions	<u>Billy</u> Y'ns	<u>Bill</u> y'ns
Defence	<u>Dee</u> fence	D'<u>fence</u>
Environment	'N <u>Vira</u> m'nt	En <u>Virun</u> Ment
Kilometre	K'<u>lomma</u> Tu	<u>Killa</u> Meeta
Maroon	M'<u>Roan</u>	M'<u>Rune</u>
Millions	<u>Milly</u> y'ns	<u>Mill</u> Y'ns
Offence	<u>Off</u> ence	U <u>fence</u>
Pornography	P'<u>nog</u> ruffy	Poor <u>nog</u> ruffy
Recycling	R'<u>cycling</u>	Ree <u>Cycling</u>
Research	<u>Ree</u> search	R'<u>search</u>
Schedule	<u>Sked</u> y'l	<u>Shed</u> y'l
Vulnerable	<u>Vunn</u> r'bul	<u>Vull</u> n'r uble

CHAPTER 13
How weeds can save the world

I dream of a future where our native wildlife are abundant around homes and in our cities. We have many of the world's most spectacular birds in Australia, but every year their numbers seem to decline. As suburbia and cities sprawl, the areas where birds can survive get smaller and smaller. Finches like the beautiful Gouldian finch face extinction. Surely we can do better.

We can. *You* can. There are things you can do to help our birds, but you will need to embrace some strange ideas. You will need to learn to love weeds–I have. Weeds can save many of our birds, especially finches.

I admire weeds. They survive where nothing else can. They resist disease, insect attack, grazing animals and people with weed killers. Weeds are here to stay. Most weeds can never be eradicated nor can some be controlled. We need to learn to live with them, not poison our planet with herbicides in a vain attempt to try to kill them.

Some weeds have been singled out by our finches as you-beaut plants. They set abundant seeds over a long period and are reliable food plants. These weeds lead a wretched life scrounging around the edges of crop areas or on waste land. Yet countless thousands of native finches rely on them for life. What if people like you and me tried to spread these weeds. Weeds grow in lots of places already.

What if we replaced the bad, useless weeds on our land with good weeds? Weeds that feed birds. These plants are vastly better at surviving and feeding birds in suburban and farming areas. And what better plant to beat a weed than another weed.

But there are those who do not like this sort of thinking. They see things differently. Ursula Hardwicke works for Wild Animal Rescue Patrol Enforcement Division (WARPED). She saves countless wild animals each year, but she can't stand it when ordinary people interfere. Ordinary people have no skills and the animals don't belong to them anyway: they belong to Warped. Warped met with the state government and had a law passed that said if they can't rehabilitate an animal to the wild, then it must be killed.

Only God and Warped can control animals, and no ordinary person can keep an animal in captivity. Recently Ursula encountered an appalling case of a magpie that fell from its nest and was saved by Jenny and Bruce Novak. They raised the bird and let it go, but it chose to stay in their yard as a pet. It couldn't fly too well and it loves Jenny and Bruce. Cheeky (the magpie) talks like a human and even plays with Schnoozie the schnauzer cross poodle. Jenny and Bruce are ordinary people and when Ursula heard of this cruelty to the magpie, she confiscated Cheeky and had him put down immediately. 'Who do these people think they are?' Ursula said.

R.I.P. Cheeky. This is the law in New South Wales.

Ursula also opposes feeding wild birds. Only Warped can feed wild animals, not ordinary people. She says feeding wild birds spreads diseases and ordinary people don't know how to do it. This causes dietary problems she says.

My turn

When Ursula saves baby joeys and echidnas from death after their mums have been run over, she is a saint. We need more of these life-savers. But (can you hear my teeth gritting?), all the rest of her views and actions are lunacy.

Many animals are rescued each year by ordinary, kind people. There are no records, but it could well be that ordinary people rescue more wildlife each year than Warped do. Some of these animals have broken wings or legs and can't be released when they have recovered. Many of them make excellent pets and live long and happy lives. As long as the government doesn't find out about them. Why Warped is so territorial about wild animals totally confuses me.

Feeding wild birds has produced large population growth in rainbow lorikeets, many rosellas and many native pigeons and doves. When Jim Cook arrived in 1770, rainbow lorikeets were uncommon birds that followed the flowering gum trees up and down the eastern coast of Australia.

Now, due to hand feeding and floriferous gardens they are residents all the way from Cairns to Melbourne. There would easily be 100 times more of these birds now than there were in 1770.

So much for the bad nutrition and diseases. Rainbow lorikeets have undertaken a long journey into the future. They feed on our verandas, inside homes, from dishes in our hands and from our garden plants. They are so smart that they have chosen to roost in groups in shopping centres up and down the coast. They chatter away and go to sleep in trees where the shopping centre lights protect them from owls, hawks and other predators. These super-smart birds are adapting to change. And change is accelerating.

If our wildlife is to have a chance of surviving into the future, it will happen on private land. Most of Australia is privately owned. National parks are maybe a tiny 6 per cent of our land area. It's up to you, me, and all the other ordinary people to save our animals even if you need to break the law to do it.

I've seen red-rumped grass parrots filling the niche normally filled by sparrows. They were eating bread scraps in the grounds of a hospital. I've seen yellow-bellied sunbirds breeding in garages. We had willy wagtails breeding on a fluorescent light in our barn. Green tree frogs live in many houses, as do geckoes. Spiders now live in car wing mirrors. Snakes, possums and goannas live inside house roofs. The list is almost endless.

Australia is changing. Our plants and animals are changing. We really must work with our plants and animals to help them adapt. In particular, we need to give them time to adapt. Not all of them are as smart as rainbow lorikeets.

If you feed finch seed to the local finches, pigeons, doves and small parrots, they have a chance of survival. If you don't, they will die. We have chopped down many of their food shrubs and trees. We have removed, grazed on or mown their grasses—therefore little seed remains. There is no wild mystical place that they can go to when the wild food in your area is gone. All the niches where there is food are already full of birds.

So they rely on us. So many ordinary people feed these birds now, that even when they go on holidays, plenty of food is still around at the houses of the people who are at home.

As the birds hang around, much like feral sparrows and pigeons, they will learn to survive better and better in suburbia. If Ursula had her way, in the fast-approaching future, our gardens will only support feral sparrows, pigeons, Indian mynahs, starlings, blackbirds and all of the other flying rats (ie. the only ones that already know how to live in the suburbs). No native birds.

So let's now ignore Ursula and concentrate on living with our native creatures. Living in harmony with our wildlife and *change*. We must not fear change, we must work with it and therefore maximise its positive effects.

Birds

A + B: Glossy Black Cockatoos are regulars in my backyard. You might note that ALL cockatoos are left-footed, they only hold food in their left foot, not the right.

I live in an indigenous native garden. We have few or no feral birds. They choose not to come because the design of my garden is repugnant to them. (See Chapter 11). The native species love it and we have more than 200 species of them. From Glossy Black Cockatoos to Goshawks to Golden Whistlers to Wonga Pigeons to Eastern Spinebills to King Parrots and so on.

Nectar feeders love: Grevilleas, banksias, kangaroo paws, paperbarks, gum trees, bottlebrushes, hakeas, waratahs.

A + B: Bottlebrushes and waratahs are also adored by nectar-feeding birds.

C: Nectar-feeding birds love grevilleas. This one is Grevillea 'Honey Gem'.

Seed eaters love: Wattle seeds, she-oak seeds, gumtree seeds, banksia seeds. But the finches love weed seeds like: guinea grass, panic veldt grass, summer grass, barnyard grass, winter grass, water couch grass.

Double bar finch.

Insect eaters love: Unsprayed plants, compost heaps, tea trees, gum trees and most local native plants.

I feed finch seed to about 1000 or so native finches, doves, parrots, pigeons every day. Don't forget to plant some dense plants for nesting in. Lilly pillies are good as are any dense native bushes.

A: Use less sprays, chuck in some natives and build a compost heap and soon your garden will be home to gorgeous insect eaters like this Pardalote.

B: Lilly pillies are attractive and dense plants that birds love to nest in.

Frogs

Do very well in gardens with rocks and ponds. They sometimes live in our toilets (Peron's tree frogs) and they breed in our ponds with native rainbow fish.

Geckoes

Love thin cracks between rocks—they live in these. They eat some of my termites that I keep for the finches. They also steal my mealworms, but I don't resent it. They live in or under our house.

Snakes

We have many carpet snakes in our roof. They control the rats and mice. They are over 2m long, but they are harmless.

We have bandicoots too. Not so many of them left. Why not act together in your neighbourhood to preserve the wildlife. You could make a huge difference. Australia is unique. We have indigenous bush and animals around all capital cities in Australia. This is virtually unheard of in the rest of the world. In New York, London, Paris or Rome–almost nothing remains of the wild animals and plants. We still have them.

The great mistake the Conservation movement made was to fight change. Far better to fight the small percentage of change that you can prevail over, then to work with change everywhere else. Thus we need to work with animals to give them enough time to adapt to a new world. To live in suburbs and towns. And yes, as a replacement for predation, this also implies population control.

Excess roof possums in cities and suburbs should be euthanased. This will stabilise their population and keep people on side with possums. If people grow to hate our wildlife, then we could lose many more species.

The conservation movement has also been pretty dopey in relation to weeds. When I approached the New South Wales government about 1980 to create Environmental Weeds Legislation, the conservation movement wasn't interested. Once the Minister Jack Hallam and I got it passed into law, the crazies came out of their burrows.

They wanted privet and lantana and camphor laurels and many other plants declared noxious. Brain dead, these weed Nazis. You could spend billions of dollars trying to eradicate these very common weeds, you could poison the whole of Australia with herbicides and you still wouldn't beat them. Better to declare these plants honorary Australian natives. Then spend the money and time on beating the weeds that can be beaten. The first two that I picked were the rhus tree and pampas grass. These two were declared noxious and are no longer a real threat.

It is a bit sad, but lantana is now a native plant, like it or not. It occurs in vast numbers on private land, and in rainforests. Many native species of birds use it as food, shelter and for nesting sites. The native birds eat the fruit and spread the seeds over huge distances as they defecate. There is an excellent argument for removing lantana and other weeds from a few prestige areas. Display areas for tourists, school kids and scientists.

But you could never stop the really nasty weeds from growing over vast areas (perhaps with the exception of biological control: it worked with prickly pear but was a disaster with cane toads and Indian mynahs). The huge savings that would occur if you ignore lantana, privet, etc. could be spent on really nailing some of the more beatable weeds.

Earlier in this chapter, I mentioned grassy weeds for wild finches. The weed Nazis get really upset about this sort of thing, but many weed grasses are now pivotal for survival of native finches in many areas.

I went to Theodore, a cotton town in Queensland. The cotton industry has eaten up most of the bushland and I expected to see few birds. I was wrong. Huge numbers of native finches populate the area. Zebra finches, double-bars, redheads, chestnuts and others. I couldn't figure it out. The conservationists say cotton farmers are destroying the land, so what gives?

I went down to the river and saw vast weedy areas of guinea grass. This weed seeds all year round in warmer zones and most of the year in temperate areas like Sydney. Clouds of finches were floating in and out of the guinea grass—a foreign invader. The finches were living off this plant and there were virtually no other seeding grasses in the area.

I can just see Dwayne Doogood, the weed Nazi from the local council going down to the river one day and spraying all of the weedy guinea grass with herbicide. Dwayne could kill tens of thousands of our precious finches in one day. Australia is changing—we must adapt as our plants and animals are.

I have tried to re-grow and regenerate native grasses. Mostly I have failed. Around heavily cropped areas or around homes, native grasses don't fare well. They usually prefer poor soils, low fertility, dry conditions, the freedom to set seed and a bushfire to start the cycle anew. In urban and farming areas the soils have been improved, we have fertilised, the conditions are fairly moist, we mow seed heads off and prevent bushfires. Native grasses tend to peter out in these situations: but weeds love them. Weeds are pre-adapted to colonise these well-watered, fertilised and cultivated areas.

Be very clear on this: in many areas, if these weeds weren't there, there would be no finches. Their native grasses that they fed on have died out as farming and houses spread. How fantastic that our native birds are smart enough to start feeding on new plants: weeds. This means they have a chance of survival.

I now grow guinea grass in Sydney. My aviary birds, finches, budgies and doves consume the green seeds with glee. My wild finches (yes <u>mine</u>, I own them since I am an Australian) feed on this weed every day in my garden.

There is an area near Windsor in NSW where they grow turf grass along the Hawkesbury River. They use vast amounts of fertiliser and herbicides and other chemicals as all turf grasses do. The land around the turf farms is severely degraded. Dwayne Doogood's brother Dougal, who is the local weed Nazi in Windsor, would put these bastards (the turf-growers) out of business if he could. They have degraded their land and created a biological desert.

Or have they? Contrary to Dougal Doogood's thoughts, vast numbers of finches live in this degraded pocket. Plumhead finches, zebra finches, redheads, doublebars and chestnuts all visit this area along with the European Goldfinches (surely an honorary native by now?). They feed on special weeds that colonise degraded, over-watered and over-fertilised land such as summer grass, barnyard grass and Johnson grass in particular. God help these poor little buggers if Dougal ever gets his way and sprays all the weeds.

I know of a farmer who was growing millet to feed pet birds. Clouds of finches descended on his crop to eat to their hearts' content. But on closer inspection they were ignoring the millet and eating a crop weed: barnyard grass. So he started growing barnyard grass and did very well out of selling it to bird breeders. And growing weeds is 10 times easier than growing a normal grain crop.

Sometimes, just sometimes, can't we look at a changed area and ask: 'What is this area now? Is it valuable or not?'. The definition of 'value' changes with time.

Panic veldt grass is a nasty weed in many areas, yet it produces seed all year for finches and seeds quite well in the shade (useful for extra seed production in dense areas). Winter grass provides useful food in winter for finches and parrots. What's wrong with this? Shouldn't we re-appraise the status of these weeds in line with their usage by our native fauna? Don't ask a weed Nazi.

But, you can do lots to rectify what Dwayne and Dougal do. Grow useful weeds. Break the law if necessary. Grow local native plants. Feed the lorikeets, other parrots, native pigeons and finches. Leave room for lizards; keep the dogs and cats away from them. Put in frog ponds. You really can make a difference.

Frogs? One last true story about a fellow ratbag. This name is real, Lance Jurd. He worked at the Riverstone Meatworks. He is a brilliant, self-taught naturalist. He noticed that the green and golden bell frog population in the creek near the meatworks was huge. Imagine that? Rare native frogs proliferating in pollution. Imagine the blood and guts that must filter out of a meat works.

Maybe the resulting algal bloom in the creek fed the taddies. Maybe the huge number of insects that would breed in this sort of degraded land would feed the mature frogs. Yeah, I know. You've all been told that frogs die in polluted areas. Whatever…

Back to reality. Lance thought, if they thrive in the wetlands around the Riverstone Meatworks, why wouldn't they thrive around the Homebush abattoirs, which also has polluted wetlands. So, this cunning naturalist took a load of the green and golden bell frogs that he had bred at his home to the Homebush site and released them.

*Lance Jurd (yes that's his real name)
and a green and golden bell frog.*

A + B: Green and golden bell frogs.

Crank the clock forward over 10 years and it was time for the Sydney Olympics…and crash! Everything had to stop at the Homebush site. A rare, indigenous population of the endangered green and golden bell frog was discovered! The usual trendy scientists heralded this as a relict population…all the usual guff. And they were preserved.

Along the way, they all missed the point that the frogs were surviving *because* of pollution (and Lance Jurd), not in spite of it. They missed also an Order of Australia for ratbag naturalist Lance Jurd. Dick Smith didn't: when no-one was looking he sent him a wad of dough to enable him to continue his work. I guess that makes Dick a ratbag too.

I am sure many of you 'ordinary Australians' (like Lance Jurd, Dick Smith and me) have seen similar things that defy the stultifying politically correct conservation dogmas that we are all fed. If you have uplifting stories of survival, change and inventiveness, please send them in to us at thelazygardener@burkesbackyard.com.au. We ordinary Aussies do own the land. It will live or die by what we do, not by what government does. And certainly, as they stand at the moment, the conservation groups are more of a threat to our ecosystems than they are a blessing. It is up to the rest of us to make a difference.

For those of you who want to give it a try, here follows my list of hero weeds.

A + B: Barnyard grass.

The hero weeds

Barnyard grass (*Echinochloa crus-galli*)

We have already heard about barnyard grass. (*Echinochloa crus-galli*) A roadside and crop weed over most of Australia. You typically find it in moist spots in or adjacent to disturbed land. That is, in or next to ploughed areas or on roadside areas scraped by a road grader. The grass grows around 1m (3ft) tall and is rather spindly (as distinct from dense). Like many of the weeds it loves the extra water and fertiliser associated with run-off from agriculture.

Seed heads are often a greenish-purple and the shed seeds are a soft brown colour. Note that each branch of the seed-heads is itself a singular unbranched spike. Spikes are usually up to 8cm (3in) long and you normally get around 10–15 spikes per seed head. You can get over 20 spikes under good conditions.

If you can't identify any of the grasses, please talk to a local farmer or perhaps ask your local council if their weeds officer can help you identify some weeds. Finches, budgies and small parrots just adore the seeds of barnyard grass, they even prefer it to most normal bird seeds.

Barnyard grass germinates in late winter to early spring and sets seed from summer into winter. It is an annual.

Guinea grass
(Panicum maximum)

Guinea grass (*Panicum maximum*)
I love this stuff. It grows so easily, you just sow some seed or pinch a plant and once your first plant grows, it pops up everywhere. It is not likely to really get out of control and it is easy to remove if you need to.

Guinea grass normally grows around 1.5m tall (but up to 2 or 3m) and forms a fairly graceful and dense clump. It is a perennial (grows for more than a year).

It sets seed all year round, but most of it is produced in the warmer months (October to May). In Queensland it sets seed even longer due to the warmer weather.

Two types of seed head are common. One has green seed heads and the other one has purple/red seed heads. Finches prefer the purple/red variety. I am not sure if there are two different forms of the plant, or if the red seed heads have just had more time and sun. Whatever, the red ones are better. This is by far the best aviary and garden plant for feeding finches. Plants can be dug up fairly easily. Cut the top back to a height of about 30cm (12in) and try to retain at least some green leaves. Pot the plant up into a normal potting mix or plant it straight into the garden. Provide some shade and daily watering for about two weeks. Do not plant a dug-up plant straight into an aviary as the birds may chew it to death. Give it four to six weeks of establishment before you let the birds at it.

Summer grass (*Digitaria sanguinalis*)
Gouldian finches love this grass. Makes them horny. Finches need the correct conditions before their sexual organs swell up and start to work. For most of the year their testes and ovaries shrink away to around one thousandth of their functional size, to save weight.

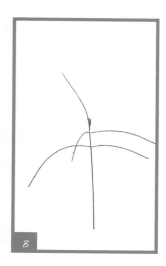

A + B: Summer grass (Digitaria sanguinalis).

Summer grass helps get them active again. Summer grass usually sets seed from December to May. It is a roadside and disturbed ground weed and it is an annual. It is a low-growing grass, more or less a groundcover with soft slightly hairy leaves. The seed heads look a bit like the framework for an umbrella and normally stand around 70cm (27in) tall. Each seed head usually has from about 5 to 8 branches (spikes). The plant and the seed heads may grow taller if clumped together under good conditions or shorten when separated in full sun and poor conditions. The leaves may colour purple as cooler weather comes. Occurs in all states but not commonly in Queensland. Budgies and small parrots love this grass.

Panic veldt grass (*Ehrharta erecta*)

Common as a garden weed in New South Wales and Victoria this is a very useful plant. It has soft, light green leaves which are very dense at ground level and the seed heads grow to around 40cm (16in) tall. Often the seed heads look like a single tall spike, but if you look closely, the branched spikes just sit against the erect main stem of the seed head. This one is very important because it both grows in the shade and seeds all year round. Unfortunately it does not set huge

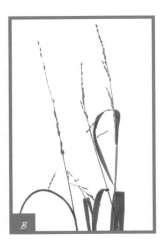

A + B:
Panic veldt
grass
(Ehrharta
erecta).

amounts of seed. It is a perennial and likes dampish spots in shade or sun. Most small birds (finches and parrots) love it.

Panic veldt grass is regarded as a very nasty weed by National Parks people. Nonetheless it is a harmless enough weed around houses and it is so widely spread that we could never eradicate it anyway.

Winter grass (*Poa annua*)

This is a godsend in winter. It is a tiny grass that is a weed in lawns and gardens in most areas of Australia. The seed heads usually only stand less than 30cm tall and the fine, soft leaves form a tuft usually around 10cm tall. The silvery-green branched seed head is well known to gardeners. Finches, budgies and small parrots love the seed heads.

Winter grass likes moisture and tolerates some shade. It seeds through winter until about December.

Winter grass (Poa annua).

A + B:
Johnson
grass
(Sorghum
halepense).

Johnson grass (*Sorghum halepense*)

This is a wild sorghum grass found in dampish spots near roads and cultivated land. It is a tall grass, growing 2–3m (6.5–10ft) high. The ripe seed heads are reddish-coloured from the distance and gracefully drooping. It is widespread across all but the colder areas of Australia. The seeds are shiny and black and about the size of a small match-head. This is too nasty and vigorous a weed to contemplate spreading or growing on purpose. You could restrict yourself to harvesting its seed heads from roadside areas. I am told that finches love its seeds. My budgies and finches don't go crazy over the seeds, but then they are very well fed. *Sorghum halepense* is declared noxious in New South Wales. The declaration states it 'must be fully and continuously suppressed'. It is a 'Prohibited Plant' in Western Australia and a Class C Noxious plant in the Northern Territory.

So what about it? Can you learn to admire weeds. For their pioneering and survival skills but most of all for their ability to nurture our wildlife. To repeat my point: most weeds are here to stay. To even try to get rid of them you would all but destroy our planet. So why not use them?

Remove useless weeds and replace them with varieties that provide food for finches. And do remember to leave areas on your property where the grasses can grow tall and set seed. This is especially important if you adjoin bushland or if you know that native finches are nearby.

CHAPTER 14
Evil angels

*T*o some people all plants are angels. Not to me. Some are truly lovely, with beautiful flowers or foliage. Or they have a wonderful perfume or they just do a job really well.

But there are those other bastards. Bastards that crack the paths and house foundations. Bastards that give you a horrific rash (rhus trees). Bastards that drop huge limbs on the house. But you do have to admire them—plants with a sense of humour or just amazing courage. Plants that, like Rhett Butler in *Gone with the Wind* proclaim: 'Frankly my dear, I don't give a damn!'

I love African violets. They cost all of $5.99 for a small one, yet they manage to take over your life, like one of those wretched Maltese dogs. These violets force you to pamper them, to nurse them and to worry about them. For $5.99. Chuck the bastards out when they have given you a few weeks of fun. Leave the guilt stuff to the Catholics.

If you must grow African violets, treat them mean. Don't water them—neglect the wretches. In winter, keep them quite dry and rarely fertilise them. Water them from below so that they don't get enough. Keep them in a brightly lit spot so that everyone can watch them suffer. Avoid direct sun, though—you want them to suffer, not die.

Are you one of those people who loves everyone? Then why did you buy this book? I am working on my life's list of enemies. You should read Chapter 24 of Volume 187. There are some right bastards in

that chapter. Drop me an email and I'll get that volume out of the freezer and send you a copy. But I digress. We all hate someone—come on, you know you do. Look, get up right now and collect some of the names from your freezer. Now, why not give one of them a really nasty plant as a gift.

Enjoy African violets until they start to look crook, then chuck the bastards out.

What about a Hill's weeping fig (*Ficus microcarpa var hillii*)? Or even a weeping fig (*Ficus benjamina*)? These despicable plants send roots out over vast distances, as far as 100m or more, just looking for trouble. Their roots block pipes, crack paths, driveways, roads and houses. Both develop gigantic canopies, often two or three blocks of land across. Surely, someone deserves one of these mongrels?

Send them a couple of packets of tulip bulbs and tell them they are easy to grow and will come up year after year. As if.

Give one a brown boronia, and say, 'Bill, this plant is really easy to grow, if you can't grow this, you can't grow anything!' Boronias, of course, cark it within 17 minutes of arriving home.

But nothing equals a rhus tree. Most people will become seriously allergic to this tree. It has glorious orange/red autumn foliage colours. People get a rash, massive swelling and skin discolouration. See how they like that.

Perhaps even the rhus is unable to compete with the lovely native rainforest tree *Dendrocnide excelsa*, aka the giant stinging tree. This monster produces large leaves covered in hair-like glass spines filled with awful toxins. Brush past the leaves, the spines are left embedded in your skin. The pain lasts for months and seriously debilitates people, dogs and other animals. Early explorers' horses are recorded as going berserk and running off cliffs to their death due to the pain. Maybe send some seeds or a leaf in the mail…

Rhus trees turn bright red in autumn, and most people are seriously allergic to this tree.

So to break paths, houses and driveways, try:
- Any evergreen fig (*Ficus spp*–eg. rubber trees)
- Liquidambars
- Evergreen alder (*Alnus jorullensis*)
- Camphor laurel (*Cinnamomum camphora*)
- Large wattles (Large *Acacia* species–eg. *A. saligna*, *A. longifolia*)

To choke out plants underneath or around them:
- She oaks (*Casuarina* or *Allocasuarina*)
- Eucalypts (many)

Trees that drop limbs:
- Coral tree (*Erythrina x skyesii*, etc.)
- Eucalypts (some *E. citriodora*, *E. maculata*, *E.mannifera ssp maculosa*)

Trees and other plants that sucker like mad:
- Golden robinias (*Robina pseudoacacia* 'Frisia')
- Bamboo, especially golden bamboo
- Lombardy poplar–*Populus nigra* 'Italica'
- Crepe myrtle
- Wisteria (a climber, not a tree)
- Bog sage (a shrub)
- Common jasmine
- *Indigophera australis*

Golden robinias sucker like mad.

Crepe myrtles are also experts at suckering.

Tall, ugly and weedy:

Cocos palm (*Arecastrum romanzoffianum*). It grows taller than a telegraph pole, provides no leaves lower down and is a weed in many areas.

Mind you, you must admire a bougainvillea. They smother everything; giant trees, even entire houses and they produce fiendish thorns that make access and egress impossible. Most people water them well and fertilise them. Do this and you get few flowers and heaps of long razor-sharp spines. Neglect the wretched plant and it flowers all the time and has few thorns.

If you really want to wear someone down over a long period, it's hard to beat some of the early native plants that nurseries used to sell. They're all miserably drab and go half-dead and ugly, then sit around for maybe 10 years before they die. *Melaleuca armillaris* is a huge, ugly paperbark that, along with *Hakea salicifolia*, was used for privacy.

Both quickly become very open, fail to give privacy, and look awful. Perhaps the two best are two awful gum trees:

Bougainvilleas are beautiful evil angels that can smother just about anything.

- *Eucalyptus nicholii* (the willow-leafed peppermint gum) was sold as a 6m (20ft) tall attractive gum tree. It grows to 20m (65ft) or more and gets really ugly.
- *Eucalyptus scoparia* has a pretty white trunk and lovely hanging narrow leaves.

Both get a very tiny and nasty suckering insect called *Thaumastocoris peregrinus*. It causes their leaves to go a reddish colour in winter, then over a number of years the foliage gets more and more sparse and eventually the trees die. A tree injection product called SilvaShield has recently come on to the market which should help with this problem.

Maybe you just hate the local kids and dogs that take a shortcut through your garden. Stick in a crown of thorns plant (*Euphorbia milii*). This will slow down their wanderings. It has fiendishly sharp spines along its stems and it skulks around at ground level waiting for bare feet.

One of my personal favourites is the bunya pine (*Araucaria bidwillii*). It grows around 30m tall (that's 100 feet in the old money) and has prickly leaves. Right at the top it sets seed. The seeds form in a dirty big pine cone about the size of a football. They weigh around 5kg and drop like a cannonball from the top of the tree. Usually the hapless owner is totally unaware that the tree has even set seed. I

have seen at least one car with its roof caved in by a magnificent salvo from a bunya pine. The seeds are edible by the way. They are inside the cone and about golf-ball sized. They taste like chestnuts: cook them in the oven at 180°C for about 45 minutes. Add butter and eat.

The crown of thorns plant (Euphorbia milii) has fiendishly sharp spines that will stop anyone from taking a short cut through your garden.

Many plants also have nasty thorns or spines. There are hakeas that have needle leaves that would go straight through your finger. Date palms (a weed in many areas, spread by birds) have hideous spines more than 10cm (4in) long. And we haven't even mentioned our friends the cacti. You can be tweezing out minute spines for weeks after encountering one of these mongrels. Here's a list of some nasties:

- Acacias (yes, many wattles are nasty)
- Agaves (succulents)
- Araucarias (eg. bunya pine)
- Berberis
- Bougainvilleas (the double-flowering ones aren't so bad)
- Bromeliads (eg. neoregelias)
- Cedrus (the true cedars)
- Chaenomeles (flowering quinces)
- Citrus (most, but particularly the Aussie finger limes)
- Crataegus (European hawthorns)
- Cycads
- Epacris (native heath)
- Grevilleas (lots: 'Canberra Gem', *dielsiana*, *x gaudichaudii*, *juniperina*, 'Pink Pearl', *rosmarinifolia*, 'Scarlet Sprite')
- Hakeas
- Junipers
- Mahonias
- Opuntia (prickly pear)
- Pereskia (climbing cactus)
- Phoenix (date palms)
- Pyracanthas (firethorns)
- Roses
- Yuccas (avoid elephantipes, it isn't at all nasty)

Prickly pears are covered in spikes and grow really big.

Now, we must move on from our rage and hatred. We are going to look at plants that may pose a risk to you and your family, or even your family's pets. So those nasty little sods really are best avoided or at best, used carefully.

Plants that cause allergies

Australia is the compromised immune system capital of the world. Lack of early exposure to dirty conditions with bacteria, etc. (ie. obsessive cleanliness with our babies) has led to compromised immune systems. According to recent research, when the immune system has nothing to do, it attacks its own body, creating allergies to many things and diseases such as diabetes. Lack of regular exposure to sunlight also disrupts the immune system since Vitamin D3 is used by the body to regulate the whole shebang.

So in the glorious land of Oz you can be allergic to anything from peanut butter to your cat. Below are some of the plants that can cause allergies. This is a rogue's gallery of the worst offenders, not a comprehensive list since almost every plant causes problems with someone.

Wattle often gets blamed for causing allergies, but in general it is harmless. It just flowers at the time when your allergies (sneezing, etc.) are bad. A few uncommon cases of wattle allergy do exist though.

Asthma weed (*Parietaria judaica*) is nasty. It grows in cracks in walls and in concrete in city areas. It has sticky leaves and its pollen upsets lots of people. It is a problem in Perth, Adelaide, Melbourne, Brisbane, Sydney, Wollongong, Newcastle and many other areas.

Asthma weed (Parietaria judaica): The pollen of this sticky weed upsets a lot of people.

Many people are allergic to moulds, so these people should not turn the compost heap. All compost heaps contain natural moulds. Allergic people should ask another family member to do the compost.

Plants known to trigger allergic reactions from asthma to hayfever include:

Grasses–most grasses produce pollen which floats in the air and causes problems. Rye grass is nasty, but almost all seeding lawn or pasture grasses are a worry. Pollen can blow in on the wind from huge distances away.

Trees like privet, mulberry, olives, liquidambars, oaks, ash, plane trees, birches, poplars, maples, cypresses and other conifers.

Other plants causing hay fever are asthma weed, Paterson's curse and plantain.

Some plants cause contact allergies such as grevilleas like 'Robyn Gordon', many tropical hybrids of *Grevillea banksii* such as 'Misty Pink', 'Pink Surprise' etc. The silky oak, *G. robusta*, also causes contact allergies, as do the rhus tree, *Primula obconica*, chrysanthemums and other daisies and euphorbias. Contact allergies usually manifest themselves as rashes, general skin allergies and swelling.

But as was mentioned, you could be allergic to your cat, your laundry detergent or your wife's perfume. Readers should note that everyone needs a wife, not just men.

Some low allergy plants are: plants with brightly coloured flowers since these are usually bird or insect pollinated and therefore aren't wind pollinated. They don't produce pollen that floats in the air. Also consider abelia, citrus, crab apple, gardenia, magnolia, plumbago, prunus, rhododendron, roses, rosemary, yucca, weigelia, camellia, lavenders, citrus, azaleas, tibouchinas, petunias, pansies, violets, anemone, begonia, bulbs (daffodils and jonquils), coleus, columbines, snow-in-summer (*Cerastium tomentosum*), verbena, ageratum, alyssum, cornflower, foxglove, larkspur, lobelia, nasturtium, nemesia, phlox, snapdragon, sweet William, and verbena. Most native plants are also excellent, but go easy on grevilleas. Plants such as *Agonis flexuosa*, banksias, bottlebrushes (*Callistemon*), cabbage palms, eucalyptus, lilly pillies, melaleuca, native violets, tea tree and westringia. Sir Walter lawn is also low allergy.

Herbs: basil, chives, dill, fennel, horseradish, marjoram, mint, oregano, parsley, rosemary, sage, thyme.

Do consult your GP if you have allergy problems and each state has an Asthma Foundation. Phone 1800 645 130 to contact your state group.

Dr Mark Ragg has written an excellent book called *The Low Allergy Garden*: Hodder Headline Australia, 1996. ISBN 0733602657. It costs around $20.

Plants poisonous to people
Dangerous if eaten:

- Angel's trumpet (*Brugmansia*): The flowers can cause hallucinations and severe poisoning.
- Cycads: The seeds are bright red and yellow and are poisonous.
- Dumb cane (*Dieffenbachia*): If any part of this indoor plant is eaten it can cause the mouth to become irritated and swell up.
- Mushrooms and toadstools: Some species are extremely toxic, others are not, so keep kids away at all times, to be safe.
- Oleander (*Nerium oleander*): All parts are poisonous but taste awful. Sap is a skin irritant.
- Poinsettia: The sap is also an irritant.
- Rhubarb leaves: The stalks are edible but the leaves contain a toxin.

Fly agaric (*Amanita muscaria*), a poisonous mushroom. Distinguishing which mushroom or toadstool varieties are toxic and which are not is quite difficult, so keep the kids away at all times to be safe.

- White cedar (*Melia*): Yellow seeds are toxic.
- Yellow oleander (*Thevetia peruviana*): Seeds are very poisonous—this plant is a major garden danger, so don't allow children near it, or get rid of the plant altogether.
- Yesterday today tomorrow (*Brunfelsia* spp.): The seeds are poisonous, and particularly so for dogs.

Technically poisonous, but usually okay

You'll find these on lists of poisonous plants but the poisonous bit is either hard to get at (eg. an underground root) or awful to eat, and no-one tries to eat it.

- Agapanthus: Underground parts
- Amaryllis: Bulbs
- Arum lily: Bulbs
- Azaleas and rhododendrons: Could be a danger to stock such as goats, sheep and cattle.
- Daffodils (*Narcissus*): Bulbs
- Foxgloves (*Digitalis*): Contains the heart medicine digitalis.
- Lily-of-the-valley: Bulbs

What to do in an emergency

Keep the Poisons Information Centre phone number, 13 11 26, near your phone.

Symptoms of poisoning from plants can include vomiting, stomach cramps, irregular heartbeat, burning to the mouth, and convulsions. The most common problems are stinging around the mouth, and skin allergies. If you do suspect a child has eaten something poisonous, important first aid measures include:

- For skin contact—gently wash the skin with clear running water.
- For eye contact—irrigate the eye with clear running water for 20 minutes.
- For swallowed plants—remove any remaining plants and wash out the child's mouth.

If you need to go to hospital, take a piece of the plant with you if you can.

Plants poisonous to dogs and cats

- Anemones or windflowers (*Anemone coronaria*)
- Bulbs (daffodils, tulips, jonquils, snowdrops)
- *Caladium bicolour* (indoor foliage plant)
- Castor oil plant (*Ricinus communis*)
- Chalice vine (*Solandra maxima*)
- Cherry tree (*Prunus serrulata*)
- Clematis (*Clematis* sp.)
- Cotoneaster (*Cotoneaster glaucophylla*)
- Cycads (notably their seed pods)
- Daffodils (*Narcissus*)
- Daphne (*Daphne odora*)
- Delphinium
- Devil's ivy (*Epipremnum aureum*)

A: *Anemones or windflowers (Anemone coronaria).*

B: *Clematis (Clematis sp.).*

- Dicentra (*Dicentra spectabilis*)
- Dieffenbachia
- Euphorbias (poinsettias, *Euphorbia characias wulfenii*)
- Food around the house: ie. apricot kernels, avocados, chocolate, grapes, macadamia nuts, onions, potatoes, raisins and sultanas are all potentially poisonous to pets
- Foxglove (*Digitalis purpurea*)
- Golden robinia (*Robinia pseudoacacia* 'Frisia')
- Hellebore (*Helleborus orientalis*)
- Hemlock (*Conium maculatum*)
- Holly (*Ilex varieties*)
- Hydrangeas
- Indoor plants: many are poisonous to pets, so keep all indoor plants out of the reach of puppies and kittens especially, but also adult dogs and cats
- Iris
- Jerusalem cherry (*Solanum pseudo-capsicum*)
- Jasmines (the climbers)
- Junipers (*juniperus sabina*) also several others

A: Foxglove
(Digitalis purpurea).

B: Hydrangeas.

- Lantana (*Lantana camara*)
- Lilac (*Syringa* varieties)
- Liliums (especially dangerous to cats)
- Madagascar jasmine (*Stephanotis*)
- Mountain laurel (*Kalmia* varieties)
- Mushrooms and toadstools
- Nightshade (*Solanum nigrum*)
- Oaks (*Quercus* varieties)
- Oleanders (*Nerium oleander, Thevetia peruviana*)
- Onions
- Philodendron
- Pines (eg. savin, *Juniperus sabina*, also several others)
- Poinciana (not the tropical tree, but the shrub *Caesalpinia pulcherrima*)
- Potatoes and green potatoes
- Privet (*Ligustrum* varieties)
- Pyracantha
- Rhododendrons (including azaleas)
- Rhubarb (leaves)
- Snowdrops (*Galanthus*)
- Snowflakes (*Leucojum*)
- Strelitzias (*Strelitzia reginae, S. nicolai*)
- Sweet peas
- Toadstools
- Tomatoes
- Tulips
- Walnuts
- Wandering jew (*Tradescantia*)
- Wisteria
- Yesterday, today and tomorrow (*Brunfelsia*)
- Yew (*Taxus* varieties)

A: Iris.

B: Liliums (especially dangerous to cats.

C: Madagascar jasmine (Stephanotis).

D: Oleanders (Nerium oleander, Thevetia peruviana).

E: Yesterday, today and tomorrow (Brunfelsia).

Pet allergies

As my eyes and nose run and I sneeze at cats, it gives me some pleasure to remember that cats and dogs too suffer allergies to various things.

Some dogs and cats have allergic skin conditions that are made worse by shampoos. Low allergen shampoos are available.

Many dogs get skin allergies on their lower parts: on their feet, elbows, under the chin and on the groin area. This is usually an allergy to wandering jew (*Tradescantia alba*). Other tradescantias such as Moses-in-the-basket (the plant with purple under its leaves) are problems as are many grasses.

Inhaled allergies: Pets can also suffer from inhalation of pollen and plant material from weeds (eg. ragweed, sorrel, dock), trees (privet, oak, pine, birch) and grasses (couch, paspalum and fescue).

Many puppies and adult dogs die from eating the fruits of brunfelsia plants (yesterday, today and tomorrow). One recently died from eating a stephanotis fruit. It's a good idea to fence young puppies off from the garden until they are over their chewing stage. This saves both the dog and the garden.

Foods to avoid feeding to dogs and cats

Curiously pets often can't handle common human foods so avoid the following:

- Apricot kernels
- Avocados
- Chocolate
- Grapes (plus sultanas and raisins)
- Macadamia nuts
- Onions

So, no leftover pizzas with onion on them for Fido. Note that macadamia nuts are quite dangerous since dogs may accidentally swallow the whole nut (shell and all). This can lead to costly surgery to remove it.

Readers may note that this book is printed on paper made from many of the bastards of trees mentioned in this chapter. Vengeance is sweet.

CHAPTER 15
The killing fields

*T*here's something about watching those B52s gliding over the forests of Vietnam, spewing out the agent orange. No better example of bending the whole planet to man's hand. Sheer, raw, unstoppable power over nature. Us blokes crave power: 'I love the small of napalm in the morning'.

Well, the last century did a lot of that. Over Europe, over Japan, over Pearl Harbour, over Rabaul, over Darwin. This is now a wiser century (we all hope that we are <u>over</u> it).

So as we enter the killing fields of your own garden, please note that the selections of treatments and sprays here are the gentlest and most effective remedy for garden problems that we know of.

There was a temptation to list lollywater treatments: treatments that don't really work but which make you feel better about your planetary behaviour. The temptation was resisted. What follows is a list of a handful of chemicals or organic substances you can use if you wish on your garden plants, especially those you don't eat.

I choose not to use sprays in general. It remains your choice. If a plant is sick, I usually either chop it out and replace it or improve its growing conditions or I move it.

Many plants get root disease—usually phytophthora root rot. I have no problem in using Yates Anti Rot as it is environmentally harmless and harmless to you too. I would use it on the usual brigade of fussy little prima donnas: boronias, daphne, Western Australian natives, avocados, citrus, etc. If the plant stabilises, I would use Seasol to promote new root growth. This is a benign product too.

But, if a plant is ill, check up what conditions it prefers. Boronias prefer Western Australia. Daphnes prefer Mt Dandenong. Citrus love Sydney and areas north of it. *Magnolia denudata*, olives and lavender love limestone soils (so add lime if you have acid soils). Lipstick palms love Cairns. Check up on the needs of your plant and, if it hates your area, grow something else.

Plants that are grown with too much nitrogenous fertiliser often get scale or caterpillar infestations. So stop fertilising the thing.

Many, many plants that have been well watered haven't been watered at all. Water-repellent soils and potting mixes are everywhere, but many gardeners are in denial. If a plant is sick, dig a hole beside it and have a look. Often the soil or potting mix will be dust dry–even though you have watered it all the time.

So get a soil wetting agent like Saturaid and scatter it on the surface and water it in. Nine times out of 10 your sick plant will simply need some TLC.

- If your African violet is sick–chuck it out.
- If your indoor maidenhair is sick–plant it in a shady spot in the garden.
- If your coriander is sick, replace it: what did it cost? $5. Get rid of it, you've probably had your money's worth.

For those of you who choose to spray here are the lists.

Pest	Best Treatment	My Preference
Aphids	Confidor	Hose them off and let the ladybirds eat the rest
Ants	Yates Bug Gun	Ignore them or block their way with Vaseline jelly.
Armyworm	Dipel (late in the day)	Dipel (late in the day)
Bronze orange bug Bronze orange bug.	Confidor	Confidor

Pest	Best Treatment	My Preference
Caterpillars *Lily caterpillars.*	Yates Success or Dipel	Yates Success
Citrus leafminer *Citrus leafminer.*	Pest Oil	Ignore them, they do no real harm
Fruit fly	Eco Naturalure	Eco Naturalure
Hibiscus beetle	Confidor or Mavrik	Confidor
Azalea lacebug *Azalea lacebug and thrips.*	Confidor	Confidor

Pest	Best Treatment	My Preference
Lawn beetle grubs	Confidor hose-on	Just fertilise the lawn
Mealybugs	Confidor (Nothing kills mealybugs)	Throw the plant away
Mites	Natrasoap or Pest Oil	Pest Oil
Scale Scale infestation on a rose stem.	Yates Scale Gun	Pest Oil
Pear and cherry slug	Yates Success	Yates Success
Snails Snails: A delicious feast for blue-tongue lizards.	Multiguard	Leave them for the blue-tongues
Thrips	Confidor	Confidor
Whitefly	Confidor	Confidor

Diseases

Disease	Treatment
Anthracnose mango (causes the flowers to drop off —ie. few or no fruit)	Mancozeb Plus
Bacterial disease	Kocide
Black spot	Yates Rose Gun
Brown patch (lawns)	Mancozeb Plus
Brown rot (peach)	Kocide
Damping off (seedlings)	Mancozeb Plus
Leaf curl (peach) *Leaf curl (peach).*	Yates Leaf Curl Copper Fungicide
Petal blight (azalea) *Petal blight (azalea).*	Mancozeb Plus

Disease	Treatment
Powdery Mildew *Powdery mildew on a button squash.*	Mancozeb Plus
Scab (lemons)	Kocide
Root rot	Yates Anti Rot
Rust	Mancozeb Plus

Please note, the intention in both Pests and Diseases lists is to minimise the number of sprays that you use. This is why the same chemical comes up again and again.

For myself, the only fungicide I use is Yates Anti Rot.

You could also use biological controls where you purchase 'good' bugs that are predators of 'bad' bugs. Go to www.goodbugs.org.au/suppliers for a list of sellers.

CHAPTER 16
Please don't bother to read this
(it's on grey water)

*T*his chapter is for the politically correct person who is probably outraged by the book so far. Read it, I dare you.

Your garden's bone dry, water restrictions are tight, your plants are begging for a drink, and you hear the washing machine sloshing away, cleaning the kids' footy gear. Slish-slosh, slish-slosh...gosh, it's dry out there. Surely you could tip that nice, sloshy water on your plants and give them a drink? Wouldn't hurt, could it?

Well, lots of so-called experts in the media like to advocate that using a bit of grey water won't do gardens any harm, but I'm not one of them. You'll be slowly poisoning your soil if you rely on untreated grey water. It's a potential health hazard and harmful for your local environment, too.

Shades of grey

Of course, there are shades of grey with household water. Water from toilets is classed as 'black' water, full of human wastes, and no-one would seriously think about putting that on their garden.

Kitchen waste water is usually classed as 'black' too because it can contain grease and animal fats. Sure, the tap water you use to wash your lettuce and vegies is probably okay to collect and put back on the garden, but lots of kitchen waste water from the washing up or dishwasher is full of fats, detergents and other unhealthy residues.

But water from bathrooms and laundries, that's the tempting stuff for thirsty gardeners. At first glance it doesn't look too bad, especially the final rinse water from washing clothes, or water that's just been used for a morning shower. Just a few traces of suds, and some of our 'experts' say that if you use a low-phosphorus laundry detergent you're ready to go!

Unfortunately, it's not just the phosphorus in detergents that poisons soils. Grey water is a chemical soup full of all sorts of chemical compounds, salts, microbes and other nasties, and phosphorus is just one of them. In the end, it's the salts in grey water that build up and do the long-lasting damage to soil. We're not just talking Saxa table salt from the kitchen, either. There's all sorts of salts in grey water, and they build up in soil, turning it salty.

Salty soups

You might remember from your high school science classes that the ordinary table salt we sprinkle on our chips is sodium chloride. Grey water contains sodium in many forms, rarely sodium chloride as it turns out, and all of these sodium compounds in grey water are salts. Every washing product, even the supposedly 'eco-friendly' ones, is loaded with sodium. This on its own can poison a soil and turn it 'sodic', a fancy name for salty.

You'll find sodium compounds in bleaches, detergents, cleaning agents and soaps. Many of the other parts of each sodium-based compound are broken down in soil, but the residue that remains, and which builds up steadily over time, is sodium—ie. salt. Pouring grey water on soil is just like sprinkling salt around your garden—and no-one in their right mind does that.

Buggy, too

Put grey water under a microscope and you'll see plenty of bugs there, and some of these are very unpleasant. Laundry water contains minute traces of faeces, for starters (from nappies and undies). There might be only a tiny amount left in the laundry rinse water, but put these microbes into nutrient-rich soil and they'll multiply rapidly. These microbes are the main reason grey water is classed as a big no-no for food plants, and they're also the reason that grey water should always be applied under the soil, rather than on the surface of the soil. When microbe-laden grey water is applied on top of nutrient-rich soil, the little bugs thrive and multiply rapidly. It doesn't bear thinking about what's happening in some Aussie backyards on sunny days. Poo farms.

Treatment systems

All right, I've made my point. I don't like grey water very much because it potentially could poison soils. In a country where soil salination is a huge problem in our farming regions, it seems pretty crazy to be turning our garden soils saline with grey water too. So, what are your options?

One is a grey water treatment system. These are not cheap and not ideal, but they do get rid of a lot of the nasties from grey water. However, even the best quality treated grey water that comes out of these systems isn't suitable for drinking or washing yourself. You can, however, use it on your garden, but that doesn't mean the water is actually 'good' for your garden. Even the treated water from a grey water treatment system has more salts in it than ordinary tap water, and the treated water can also be more alkaline than ordinary tap water, and some plants won't like it.

There are two different designs of grey water treatment systems in the marketplace. One is based on filtering the water with a series of sophisticated filters until the water reaches an acceptable standard. The other design is based on a biological process, where microbes break down the chemicals in the grey water. We won't go into the pros and cons of how these work, but both systems do work. There's a whole accreditation process behind them, and you'd be mad to get anything other than a fully government-accredited grey water treatment system.

A big issue of course is price. Systems vary in price from around $5500 up to $13,000 and beyond, and that doesn't include the cost of installation, which varies widely depending on your individual situation. You might be able to get a rebate from your local water authority to help defray the cost, so check that out.

A grey water treatment system is a big investment. The alternative is, of course, a water tank. A water tank will probably end up being cheaper than a treatment system, and the water quality might be better—but tanks can run dry, while the treatment systems keep on chugging along producing treated water for you, no matter how dry the weather.

Using sub-standard water

Beautiful rain falling from the sky and drinking water from our taps is the top-class stuff, the first-class water that we should give to our gardens wherever possible.

Rainwater collected in a tank is usually good enough quality water for gardens if your house roof is clean, you don't live in a polluted part of the city and you've fitted 'first-flush' devices to keep out the debris that washes off the roof with the first burst of rain after a dry spell. In urban areas tank water is definitely not top-quality drinking water for humans, but there's many a rural Aussie who has been brought up on tank water, and they swear by it.

Treated water from grey water treatment systems, no matter how good the system, ought to be thought of as second-class water for gardens because it still contains salt residues and can be more alkaline than tap water and rain water.

And if you're going to go ahead and ignore all our warnings about using grey water collected from your laundry and bathroom, let's call that third-class water for gardens. In the interests of at least slowing down the rate at which you poison your soils, here's a few tips on how to use sub-standard second and third class water.

1. Don't use sub-standard water in the same place all the time. Spread it around your garden, and make sure that wherever you applied it, the next time you water that area you use some first-class water from your tap or tank. Every part of your garden should get first-class water most of the time, and sub-standard water only occasionally. Those cheap and nasty grey water 'diversion' systems usually direct the grey water to one spot via a pipe, and that's a very bad idea.

2. If any plant that used to be healthy starts to look sick after watering it with sub-standard water, never apply the sub-standard stuff to it again.

3. Keep third-class water (ie. untreated grey water) well away from all food plants. Water from grey water treatment systems, however, is classed as being okay to use on food plants.

4. Never use untreated grey water on native plants. Most of them will just keel over and die, due to the phosphorus content in the untreated water. Lots of home owners have discovered that the supposedly 'treated' water from their septic tank systems kills their native plants.

5. Direct your sub-standard second and third-class water onto your lawn instead.

6. Take into account your soil type when using sub-standard water. Heavier soils such as clay-based soils will trap and retain salts and other nasty compounds more readily than will a free-draining, light sandy soil.

7. Third-class untreated grey water should be applied under the soil, via sub-surface irrigation pipes. Applying it to the surface of the soil will encourage microbes and other unhealthy bugs to multiply more rapidly.

8. Do buy the slightly better low-phosphorus laundry detergents (available now in supermarkets under various brands, including Planet Ark). The untreated grey water from them will at least contain less phosphorus, but it will still be loaded up with salts.

9. If your garden plants don't cope well with your substandard water, you could consider changing the plants you grow in your garden. Some plants cope better with poor quality soil and water than others, and I like to call them 'poo plants'. See my listing, below, of the best poo plants for gardens.

The bottom line
I wouldn't use untreated grey water on gardens. It slowly poisons the soil. Either change what you're growing in your garden, invest in a rainwater tank or, if you can afford it, a grey water treatment system. But I'd go and annoy your local politician too. Tell them you want

another dam built, and a water recycling scheme, all the leaky pipes fixed and covers put on all the open irrigation channels. If your pollie promises you all that, vote for them.

Best poo plants for gardens

There's no guarantee that any or all of these plants will actually survive in gardens watered with salty, sub-standard water such as grey water, treated septic tank water or even water from sophisticated grey water treatment systems. But these are your best bets. If you try them and they fail, don't persist with them. The one plant that is likely to cope with poor quality water is lawn grass. That's where your substandard water should go, most of the time, but these 'poo plants' are at least worth a try.

Natives

Names	Growth habit
Acacia floribunda – white sallow wattle	3–5m shrub or small tree
Austromyrtus inophloia 'Blushing Beauty'	2m shrub
Austromyrtus inophloia 'Aurora'	3m shrub
Banksia robur–swamp banksia	2m shrub
Callistemon varieties (most)–bottlebrush	prostrate, shrubs, trees
Carex varieties (most)–sedges	to 1m tall
Casuarina cunninghamiana–river oak	20m tree
Casuarina glauca–swamp oak	20m tree
Cordylines (most)	2–3m clumps
Crinum pedunculatum–swamp lily	2m clump
Dianella caerulea	1m clump
Eucalyptus camaldulensis–river redgum	20m tree

Names	Growth habit
Eucalyptus grandis–flooded gum	20m tree
Eucalyptus ptychocarpa–swamp bloodwood	10m tree
Ferns (most)	prostrate
Ferns, tree *Dicksonia* and cyatheas	3–8m trees
Helmholtzia glaberrima–stream lily	1–2m clump
Isotoma fluviatilis–swamp isotome	groundcover
Leptospermum scoparium–common tea tree	2m shrub
Lilly pillies (all)–*Acmena, Syzygium, Waterhousea*	1–10m shrubs/trees
Lomandra confertifolia–mat rush	low, grass-like
Lomandra hystrix–mat rush	1m grass-like
Melaleuca varieties (all)	1–8m shrubs
Palms (most)	2–20m
Pratia pedunculata	groundcover
Tristania neriifolia–water gum	3m shrub
Tristaniopsis laurina–water gum	10m tree
Rainforest species (most)	Various
Xanthostemon chrysanthus – golden penda	15m tree

Non-natives

Names	Growth habit
Acanthus mollis	1–2m clump
Acorus gramineus	30cm grassy clump
Canna hybrids	to 2m clumps
Chaenomeles speciosa–flowering quince	2–3m shrub
Colocasia–taro (all 'elephants ears' plants)	to 2m clumps
Cordyline species and hybrids	to 8m clumps
Cyperus papyrus (and dwarf species)–papyrus	0.5–2m clumps
Ferns (most)	prostrate to 8m
Gunnera manicata	2.5m clumps
Hostas (most)	40cm clumps
Hydrangeas (most)	2m shrub
Impatiens–busy lizzie	60cm shrub
Iris (Louisiana hybrids)	1.5m clump
Liquidambar styraciflua	30m tree
Nerium oleander–oleander	1–4m shrub
Nyssa sylvatica–tupelo	20m tree
Palms (most)	various sizes
Phormium tenax–NZ flax	to 2m clump
Taxodium distichum–bald cypress	20m tree
Zantedeschia aethicopia–arum	

First published in Australia in 2008 by
Reed New Holland
an imprint of New Holland Publishers (Australia) Pty Ltd
Sydney • Auckland • London • Cape Town

1/66 Gibbes Street Chatswood NSW 2067 Australia
218 Lake Road Northcote Auckland New Zealand
86 Edgware Road London W2 2EA United Kingdom
80 McKenzie Street Cape Town 8001 South Africa

A record of this book is held at the National Library of Australia

ISBN 9781877069628

Publisher: Fiona Schultz
Publishing Manager: Lliane Clarke
Senior editor: Joanna Tovia
Designer: Hayley Norman
Production Manager: Linda Bottari
Printer: SC (Sang Choy) International Pte Ltd, Singapore
Author: Don Burke (aka Clarrie)
Cartoons: Peter Meldrum
Chief Photographer: Brent Wilson
Editorial Consultant: Jamie McIlwraith
Horticultural Consultant: Geoffrey Burnie
Editorial Co-ordinator: Chris Burke
Additional photos by: Paul Broben, Simon Griffiths, Don Burke, Sarah Callister, Ashley Smith,
Mitch Bailey, Deric Werth, Chris Burke, Geoff Higgins and Photolibrary.

10 9 8 7 6 5 4 3 2